CREATING HOOKED RUGS

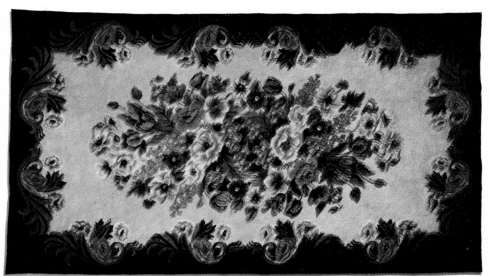

SHIRLEY POPPIES, *hooked by Mildred Smith*

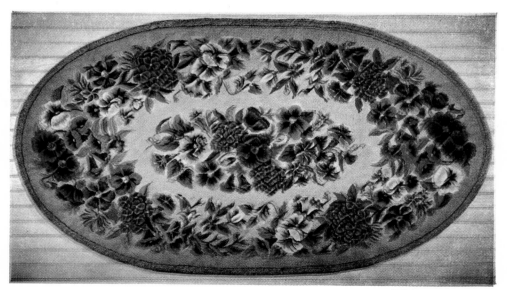

DREAM GARDEN, *hooked by Mildred Smith*

CREATING HOOKED RUGS

VERA BISBEE UNDERHILL

with

ARTHUR J. BURKS

Sketches by Florence Starr Taylor

BRAMHALL HOUSE · NEW YORK

This edition is published by Bramhall House,
a division of Clarkson N. Potter, Inc.,
by arrangement with Coward-McCann, Inc.
(A)

Manufactured in the United States of America

TO MY MOTHER
AND
TO ALL WOMEN WHO HAVE BEEN IN-
SPIRED TO CREATE BEAUTY WITH THEIR
HANDS AND HAVE SHARED IT WITH OTHERS

Acknowledgments

To Mr. and Mrs. Bruce Zeiser: I am deeply grateful for all the help and encouragement that they so willingly gave me in the preparation of this book, and for permission to use and photograph many of the Heirloom patterns.

To Mrs. Caroline Saunders, for the inspirational teaching she has given not only to me but to hundreds of other grateful pupils; also for photographic use of her patterns for this book.

To Mrs. Mildred Smith, who so graciously added many photographs of her beautiful rugs, which are not only masterpieces but truly inspirational and instructive.

To Massachusetts Extension Service for their help and co-operation.

To all of my pupils who encouraged and helped me, and whose rugs are shown in this book.

Contents

CONTENTS

Illustrations

COLOR PLATES

BLACK AND WHITE PHOTOGRAPHS
(following page 14)

ILLUSTRATIONS

(following page 30)

From a Distinguished Designer

THOSE of us fortunate enough to have learned rug hooking from Caroline Cleaves Saunders, of Clinton, Massachusetts, realize that we have had a training that cannot be acquired from books. The most important books to anyone interested in rug hooking are Mr. W. W. Kent's three volumes on Hooked Rugs. While these books give the history of rug hooking and show many illustrations of treasured old rugs, nevertheless they do not instruct women to make rugs as they are being developed today.

Vera Underhill, one of Mrs. Saunders' talented pupils, moved from New England where the craft of rug hooking is so prevalent that rug enthusiasts see rug exhibitions at all times of the year and have the opportunity to join classes in nearly every community, thereby getting help and inspiration wherever needed. Mrs. Underhill has realized, being cut off from these associations, how eagerly women elsewhere are seeking help in this fascinating craft. Not being able to personally teach all those seeking her help she has endeavored to pass on to others some of her enthusiasm and skill in the art of hooking rugs.

It is my firm belief that the ideal way to learn rug hooking is with a talented teacher rather than to struggle with the many subtleties of hooking alone, but good teachers are so rare and so inaccessible to the majority of hookers and most teachers are so much in need of guidance themselves that I feel sure Mrs. Underhill's book will be a great help not only to the novice but to many rug teachers as well.

I know of no rug hooker who does not avidly read every article on rug hooking and attend every exhibition possible in order to increase her knowledge of this craft. I am sure all hookers will find much practical help and certainly much inspiration from this book of Vera Underhill's.

—LOUISE HUNTER ZEISER

54 Irving Avenue
Providence, R.I.

What Art Means to Me

I FEEL within an impulse, perhaps that divine impulse which has moved all races in all ages and in all climes, to record in enduring form the emotions that stir within.

I may model these in clay, carve them in wood, hew them in stone, or forge them in steel. I may weave them in textiles, paint them on canvas or voice them in song, but whichever I do I must harken always to the song of the lark and the melody of the forest and stream and respond to the color of the rose and the structure of the lily, so that my creation may be in accord with God's laws and the universal law of order, perfect fitness and harmony.

Moreover I must make my creation good and honest and true so that it may live after I am dead, revealing to others something of the pleasure which I found in its making.

Then will my creation be art and whether I be poet or painter, blacksmith or cobbler, for I shall have labored honestly and lovingly in the realization of an ideal.

—C. Valentine Kirby

Introduction

What is so great a good as the joy of creating—Of shaping with
our own thoughts and hands the beauty which others may share?
—Robert Weston

IT HAS been said that almost everyone has at some time during his life
toyed with the idea of writing a book. To entertain such an idea did not
occur to me, but I was intensely interested in hooking rugs and helping
to teach this fascinating art to others. Many women outside of my classes had
asked me about books on rugmaking; not just any book, but a complete
textbook written deliberately for the novice; personal, not too technical, simple
and clear; a book that would definitely teach how the rug artist started and

worked her way into the fullest expression of the art. I knew of no such book. Most of the printed instruction material on rugmaking that I had read was comprehensible only after I had become deeply involved in the art of rugmaking. A book "bridge" seemed necessary, across the confusing territory between ignorance of rugmaking and a workable knowledge of its entrancing ramifications. This book is intended to be a chatty textbook for the novice. It is hoped that the more experienced hookers may find enjoyment and inspiration from the many sketches, pictures, and even from the text itself.

I have read many books and articles on rugmaking. There is considerable literature on the subject, for rugmaking is old and international. The spirit of rugmaking, the why of it, the inspiration of it is seldom come by. The reason is obvious: most rugmakers hesitate to commit themselves on paper because they feel that it is the rug itself, in fullest detail of color, design, size, etc., which people, especially women, wish to read about. Thus the real value of the art is left out. I do not say this to dissuade any novice from buying books and pamphlets on handmade rugs, for she needs all the literature she can find. Every piece of writing about rugs, to most ruggers, is valuable, but almost never does it contain the key to the heart of the hooked-rug artist. Handmade rugs speak a language of their own and it is a language dear to the heart of every ardent hooker. It is the heart I wish to touch, for through the heart flows inspiration. I cannot expect to touch any one else's heart without giving my own.

I have lectured on rugmaking in many sections of eastern Pennsylvania, before women's clubs, the Pennsylvania Society of Farm Women, civic groups, extension groups, and to church groups. I spoke of hooked rugmaking as "painting with wools," an idea that was new to these women in Pennsylvania. Most of the people I met had never experienced rugmaking as artistry. It seemed strange to me, coming from New England where we are steeped in the rugmaking tradition, that it should be new to so many in Pennsylvania. Interest in this craft grew rapidly and so many women came seeking to be taught that it was impossible for me to help them all. Thus the idea of a book was born.

Personally I do not claim to be an artist. Like many women I am not endowed with any great talent or ability. But for a long time I had felt that there was a crying need for a good hooked-rug textbook, especially for beginning teachers and for the novice who had no contact with a teacher or with groups of women who were already hooking. When the opportunity to write a book was presented to me I felt that here was a chance to do something for the hundreds of women who needed help in securing the kind of textbook that would serve as a teacher.

I have taught many home-economics classes, especially foods and clothing, to both teen-agers and adults. Repeatedly I have found that unless the instructions were simple, clear, and to the point, the inexperienced became confused and made mistakes. How often have you, when starting something new, like knitting, crocheting, or sewing, discovered that you could follow the instructions up to a certain point and then some detail baffled you? Either you ran to a neighbor for help, called someone on the phone to explain it to you, or, as many others have done, lost interest and tossed the whole thing in a closet and forgotten it. Most women, especially in a rug class, want the teacher to do everything for them because they are afraid to try their own ideas. To most women it is not enough to give instructions for one flower in one rug, and then leave the rest of the planning to the beginner to figure out. Women who are beginners usually want every detail planned for them. I believe that many persons who are authorities on any kind of creative work were to begin with real artists. Instructions written by such persons are usually perfectly clear to the experienced, but to the novice there is much that puzzles her and she will give up rather than try to figure it all out by herself. The artist often takes it for granted that the simple fundamental instructions are already understood and thus for the beginner much is left out that is important. It is with this thought in mind that a good textbook for the beginner needs visual instruction with sketches, good color plates (for color is the blood stream of the hooked-rug artist) as well as a complete text of instructions.

I do not wish to give the impression that my ideas are the correct way. All hooked-rug teachers may differ in their methods of teaching and while one may not be in accordance with the others, each may be correct. I only wish to point out the possibilities, sharing such knowledge as I possess with all who wish to learn. There are thousands of women who are eagerly and desperately wanting a teacher's help, but are unfortunate not to be within reach of a good hooked-rug teacher.

I, like many other women, was inspired by the teaching of Mrs. Caroline C. Saunders of Clinton, Massachusetts, one of New England's finest teachers. For over twenty years Caroline Saunders and her students have been quietly striving to restore interest in this method of artistic expression. For many women, hooking rugs becomes a "must" at first sight. They cannot rest until they know how it is done and have completed their own first rugs. Other women wish to learn, but feel that the mastery of the art is beyond them. Many women in this latter group who feel they have no artistic ability, and who know a feeling of utter helplessness when urged to display creative talent, discover to their joy and amazement a natural gift for hooking rugs. There are rugs—I see some of them every day or so among my co-workers—which, though they are the first, second, or third done by their makers, still clutch at the throat with their beauty; they are really rugs that inspire. Such rugs are within reach of any woman anywhere if she has hands and eyes. I don't mean that she may buy them, but that she may make them!

There are no heartaches in handmade rugs though at first there may seem to be. Such heartaches as beginners may discover in their first attempts to create beauty will be found, soon, to be nothing more than inspiration, stirring imagination in its sleep.

I'm an eager believer in the general co-operation by women to better their own small or large worlds. I know of nothing more efficient than a common hobby to bind them together in mutual interest; nor any hobby more inspiring than hooked rugs.

Years ago machines almost drove handmade rugs out of our national life. Machines did not destroy women of artistic inclinations. A few of them, like Mrs. Caroline Saunders, set themselves the task of preserving the beauty and tradition of the handmade rug. They gradually succeeded and because of Mrs. Saunders' efforts, this old craft has survived to a new generation with a greater interest and enthusiasm. Few women's magazines now appear for as much as a year without some reference to handmade rugs, stories illustrated by drawings or photographs of designs, particular rugs, etc.

Women fortunate enough to be taught by such an artist as Mrs. Mildred Smith of South Peabody, Massachusetts, are to be envied. In my estimation there is none better. To visit one of her exhibits and see the results of her teacher-pupil efforts is indeed inspiring. I am sure that rugs created under the supervision of such a teacher will be treasured for generations; they are indeed tomorrow's heirlooms. I believe Mrs. Smith will agree with me, however, that a pupil who has finished several rugs under a good teacher's supervision will find an even greater thrill in planning and creating her own color schemes, working out her own ideas of shading and completing rugs that are her own dreams. So many pupils lean on a teacher for every leaf, flower, and scroll without giving rein to their own imaginations, that the teacher may induce her pupils to proceed on their own as quickly as possible. Then if you are a novice and you start to develop your own ideas even on a small leaf or flower you have taken the plunge and the teacher will guide you in the development of your own ideas; these ideas are your own creative expression. Each step you take will make you wonder why you thought it to be so difficult. Before long you will find that others come to you for help and advice and you are then treated to the greatest thrill of all, the opportunity to teach, share, and learn while you teach. You may never afterward hook many rugs for yourself—time is of the essence for the teacher—but you will know the joy of giving others a chance to discover their own outlets to fulfillment.

If you have the urge to express yourself in some way that seems to elude you, you have some creative ability. There may be the merest hint of artistic ability in you, but dabbling with many colored pieces of cloth, a beautiful design on burlap, dye, simple tools, and watching a hooked rug grow under your very own hands is, I am sure, a certain way to develop your artistry beyond anything you ever hoped. This statement is based on personal experience as well as on the personal observation of the inspirational blooming of other women as hooked-rug artists.

Rug artists have but one thing against which to guard: the quickly acquired attitude that the world of feminine interest contains nothing but hooked rugs! Addiction is almost certain. No rug artist seems to care in the least what anybody thinks about her consecrated attitude toward her art. As long as she speaks a known language, even if it consists mostly of such words as "frame," "hook," "design," "burlap," "wool," "dye," etc., has anybody really any reason to complain? If anyone has, let that one discover rug artistry and assume the preferred attitude! More and more women around the nation, eager for self-expression, are rediscovering hooked rugs. Rugmaking can be worked into the family routine so easily, so naturally—as it was long ago when fireplaces and cold winter nights were in closer harmony—that not only does it not interfere with other family tasks, but complements each one and enriches its accomplishment.

Thanks to hooked rugs, the making of hooked rugs, the teaching of hooked rugmaking, I have made many friends, worth more than all else I could have attained; worth more than the finest hooked rug of my dreams. I came to Lancaster County a stranger. Hooked rugs have opened the homes and hearts of these genuinely hospitable, warmhearted, and generous Pennsylvania Dutch people. A dyed-in-the-wool New Englander has really found a second home in this beautiful rolling countryside, known as the Garden Spot of the World!

INTRODUCTION

I know of nothing more inspiring than beautiful hooked rugs to bring people together, whether the people be the family of the rug artist or strangers. Very soon after hooked rugs become the topic of mutually interesting discussion, people are no longer strangers.

—V.B.U.

CREATING
HOOKED RUGS

I. Your Own Magic Carpet

MY WORLD

God gave my world to me
And I rebelliously
    Cried out, "how small!
    And is this all?"
His words were sad, yet mild;
"All that you love, my child."

Myself that moment died,
And born anew I cried:
    "Love, take control
    And lead my soul
To serve my small estate."
And lo, my world is great!

          —C. R. PIETY

FOR most women there really is a bit of magic, in this art of hooking rugs. For once you start it seems to spread like a fever through the family and neighborhood. I, for one, can hardly wait until I have finished one pattern and started on the next one. And there are always a dozen more I want to do. I do not believe it to be a fad or a passing fancy. I know many women who intend to make it a lifetime hobby. For over twenty years New England women have been taking lessons in this method of artistic expression and each year the number of pupils continues to grow beyond the capacity of teachers. I have known many instances of women traveling hundreds of miles just to see a rug exhibit. I myself have made the trip from Lancaster to Lynn, Massachusetts, some 400 miles, just to see Mildred Smith's rug exhibit and I have always felt that it was well worth the trip. Rug exhibits are a source of inspiration and every woman who hooks enjoys going to as many of them as possible. In New England you will find a rug exhibit being held almost every week during the spring and fall. Rug exhibits offer not only a chance for teacher and pupil to display what they have accomplished in the past year, but they offer the greatest source of inspiration to other women.

A friend of mine finds hooking so fascinating that her family claim she neglects them. They have taken to leaving notes on the rug frame to remind her that Dad needs a button sewed on his shirt and Sis needs a skirt pressed! And often I have passed my rug frame while in the midst of household chores and found the temptation so great that I could not resist stopping to hook for a few minutes. The only trouble is that the few minutes become hours and the hours have flown so quickly that I have very little time to prepare dinner. How thankful I am for a pressure cooker and home-economics training!

I am continually amazed at the number of husbands who display such keen interest in their wives' handwork. Often it is the husband who is the first to rush guests to the room where the latest rug is proudly displayed or being hooked.

One of the women in my class often goes on business trips with her husband. Now that she has developed an interest in hooking rugs she prefers to remain at home so she can hook on her latest pattern. However, she has recently compromised and now takes her frame and rug along in the car and passes the hours in her hotel room hooking on her rug, and she loves it!

I read recently of an actress who was playing in a hit show on Broadway. She had a very difficult part, that of a mother who kills her two children. Because this scene was so upsetting and took so much out of her she found that the only thing which calmed her nerves and relaxed her was to return to her apartment after the show and hook for an hour or so on her latest rug.

One of the greatest rewards I have gotten from teaching is when a husband of one of my pupils stopped me one day, shook my hand and said, "I just want to thank you for all the pleasure you have given my wife in teaching her how to make such lovely rugs. She has often said that she never enjoyed anything so much."

For me there is still a more wonderful bit of magic in hooking rugs. Before teaching others how to hook flowers, I was aware only of the beauty and fragrance of the rose and the lily. I could tell you the names of the flowers in my garden and their colors, but there my knowledge and appreciation of the flowers stopped. Now I thrill not only to the beauty and the fragrance of the rose as it unfolds its dewy petals at dawn but I have become aware of its structure, the way its petals curl, its tightly closed bud and its shiny green leaves. I now notice how the leaves are veined with their various shades of green! Even the lowly pansy has become a thing of great beauty, for in its soft velvet petals are such exquisite colorings and shadings that you cannot doubt but a greater Hand than yours or mine created such beauty. I'm reminded of a verse from Tennyson:

> Little flower—but IF I could understand
> What you are, root and all, and all in all,
> I should know what God and man is.

God has surrounded us with such beauty that I am sure He meant for us all to enjoy it. To some this beauty never becomes apparent; their senses never become aware of it. I found that after hooking rugs and trying to copy nature, life suddenly took on a new meaning. I became aware of an infinite number of things that heretofore had escaped my notice. While working with the artist on this book I became even more aware of the magic of light and shadow and the beauty to be found in it. I spoke of this to the artist, Florence Taylor, who replied, "Even a garbage pail is beautiful if the light strikes it right!"

Then, too, there is a bit of magic for the woman who never felt that she was artistically inclined. She suddenly produces a bit of breath-taking beauty and realizes that she has found an outlet for her creative urge, that it was amazingly easy, and fun to do. I am positive that many women, like myself, enjoy creating beauty—but they want it to be something easy and pleasant to do.

Tradition has it that for many years New England and Canadian mothers would hook a rug for each of their daughters to stand upon when they were married. My own mother, as a bride, stood upon a rug that Grandma hooked for her. Mrs. Saunders also hooked a rug for each of her daughters to stand upon when they were married. Although this is no longer the custom, today many a bride receives a lovely hooked rug from her mother or a relative and considers it among her most prized possessions.

5

Why has the revival of an old craft created so much interest during the past few years? Almost all women's magazines carry some information on hooked rugs during their yearly publication. There are many reasons for its popularity. There is better equipment, a greater variety of materials, many more colors with which to work; and teachers willing to instruct. Because it is easy and pleasant work; it is a popular pastime hobby. Also because it is not a messy job; it can be part of the living-room furniture, as mine is; and one may drop down to the rug frame and hook for a few minutes or many hours and feel relaxed. It does not require strict concentration, especially if a teacher has already worked out the details, and thus sociability and hooking are combined. Conversation with family and friends make it a more enjoyable hobby. Perhaps for some it evolves from the very fact of civilization's increasing pace in which the routine of the housewife seems so often unrewarding. The housewife may feel that she is in a rut, that her house holds her back while the rest of the world passes her by. To many women, hooking rugs offers the perfect release, the escape from frustration. To my knowledge there is no craft that commands so much attention and praise, from beginning to finished product, from family and friends alike. Often attention and praise are like soothing balm to the average housewife, who feels that she cannot compete with career women who may also be good housewives and mothers. Radio, television, and magazine addicts, women are constantly aware via these media of the career and professional women and their increasing abilities in all fields. Often the housewife feels that she lacks opportunity to express herself and to be creative because she is so firmly tied to housekeeping routine.

So many women have said to me, "Oh, how I would love to learn how to make those beautiful rugs, but I just haven't the time to take lessons. I guess I'll have to wait until I retire or my children grow up." Well, I believe that we can always find time to do the things we really want to do. I have seen business and professional people who have given their hearts and souls to their jobs and when they retired go to pieces because they had no other interest in life. Recently a doctor made a statement to the effect that we live under such strain and tension today that we do not learn how to relax, and so, many people become mental cases. How often women allow all their leisure time to be absorbed by a dozen or more clubs and organizations. I, for one, deplore any time spent in unproductive activity. So many demands are made upon our time that we should learn to say "no" to many and offer our services to the ones that are worth while and inspiring. I believe we mothers would be under less tension and happier if we did so.

6

YOUR OWN MAGIC CARPET

It was Bryant's belief that Nature could teach us how to live:

> And to the beautiful order of thy works
> Learn to conform the order of our lives.

Today many women are learning the value of an interesting, productive, and creative hobby, and thus transforming a corner of their homes into miniature studios. Of all the crafts that are popular today, rugmaking is perhaps the most easily adapted to time and place. The frame on which the burlap is stretched and the rug hooked is light, portable, and inexpensive, enabling all women who wish to combine social activity with a worth-while hobby.

Compare this craft with weaving. I have always felt that weaving would be fascinating and rewarding but to my mind it is not the ideal hobby for every woman, regardless of station, time, and space. The weaver's loom is more expensive, needs a special room and cannot be moved from place to place except as a major operation. Certainly the loom cannot be picked up and carried to the house of a neighbor for a special afternoon, while the rug-maker's frame can be, at any desired time, whenever the mood to hook strikes.

When the rug artist has increased her circle by accepting pupils, or simply for the fun of having company, groups of women gather and combine hooking with social activity, almost any time of a given day. This is one reason for its popularity. My own group has even assembled for breakfast. We have set up our frames near enough to one another that conversation could be general, out on the lawn, under the trees, when the days were sunny. On a rainy day nothing can brighten the life of the housewife more than a gathering around the fireplace, all frames busy, conversation keeping pace with the brightness of the fire. Dyes can be bubbling on the stove or on an outdoor fireplace. All of this, except dyeing, can take place anywhere or in any room. Hooking then becomes more satisfying and inspiring than bridge or the movies. We feel that hooking time is time well spent, for we have something worth while to show for our effort.

Is this true of any other hobby? Ceramics, for example? Ceramics, too, is a fascinating hobby but the cost is higher and opportunities for entertainment are almost nil. Rugmaking can be halted anywhere at any time. This is not possible in pottery making, many phases of it being continuous or the phase is a distinct loss. The potter is tied to such phases and cannot drop them—one of the principal recommendations for rughooking. With pottery there is always fear of breakage, with resultant heartache if a firing doesn't come out right. A broken piece can't be done over. Any time or place in the making of a rug you may rip out unsatisfactory attempts and make a new start. For most women rughooking remains the ideal method of feminine self-expression.

Every woman I have met has the urge to express herself artistically. Every woman is an artist in her heart. She may never become a painter, poet, writer, singer, or composer, but resignation will never quell her urge to be something. The handmade rug is the simplest, most satisfying way to self-expression for the woman with hands, eyes, and imagination. Men and children also find handmade rugs of great interest. Edward Sands Frost, a New England tin peddler, originated the first commercial hooked-rug pattern in the United States in 1868. His patterns are still being used. Other men have proved themselves quite capable of outstanding artistry in hooked rugs. But the hooked rug is peculiarly fascinating to women, making daily routine more enjoyable.

Because it is something you do with your hands, from your own inspiration, the handmade rug expresses your own individuality. During the hooking of a given rug the growing work expresses every mood of the maker and when it is finished it *is* the maker. With your first rug you become the artist you have always dreamed of being. You can see what you have done and find it good. As you progress you become increasingly proud of your ability. Your inventiveness grows. And, to repeat, if you do not like any or all of it you can rip any or all of it out and start afresh. You have lost nothing but your time and the time during which an artist has learned something of her artistry is definitely not lost. You have learned much from your frustrations over design, color, facility of creation, the tools of your trade-hobby. You discover for one thing that your very frustrations are the labor pains of creation.

Women seldom fail to complete a rug. The problems involved, of which there are many, to be anticipated and discussed in this book, challenge the ingenuity. In many ways they are extensions and projections of the daily problems of the housewife or career woman. Since the handmade rug, done as a hobby rather than a business, is a pick-up job, it fits into the broken periods of the day or night, becoming the cement that holds the days together, the stitching that gives the hours form and meaning. A bit of hooking can be done while things are brewing in the kitchen, the clothes are washing, the children prepare lessons, or while hubby reads the newspaper. Since woman's hands quickly learn to hook, inspiration need not interfere with words and thoughts, the arrival of guests, the necessity for speech. In fact, visitors enhance the rugmaker's inspiration, since she then shows her work—proudly, too. Husbandly comment, criticism by the children, remarks of visitors and other hookers play their part in the finished product insofar as the rug-artist makes use of them. The progressive rugmaker overlooks nothing that will help her. Part of her artistry is to make use of everything that comes her way that can be used.

Just how can a handmade rug be an artistic expression? First, a design is required. It may be purchased or evolved. As far as the novice is concerned I recommend purchase. You may develop to the point where you will create your own designs, but then you are no longer that novice for whom this book is prepared! But if you select someone else's design, or pick one out of a magazine, how can it possibly be called your own? Because you select the one that appeals to you. If there are twenty from which to choose the fact that all twenty were created by someone else doesn't detract from the fact that you selected one or two, exercising artist's choice. And you have started.

Today there are more and more designers who prepare the burlap background for the hooked rug. When you select the burlap ready for hooking you have once more expressed yourself, for you have decided not only on design but size. What influences your decision on a certain size for a certain rug you plan to make? Intentionally you have picked a spot in your home that the rug will fit. How have you done this? By studying the room, or the spot, with reference to other furnishings, other rugs, and arriving at the artist's conclusion that just such a rug, of such size and design, will fit that spot!

Are you an interior decorator then? Have you ever thought you had ability in that line? Answering these two questions gives you more insight into yourself. Maybe you are an interior decorator after all! Who moves the furniture around in your home until it pleases? Who selects it in the first place? Who makes all the changes when housecleaning days are at hand? Maybe you don't give it much thought, but size, design, background, a room, a corner, a nook, a niche, all are pieces of the jigsaw puzzle of your artistic plan into which you fit the rug you are making.

The painter mixes his pigments; so does the rugmaker and your pigments are considerably more varied than those of the painter. You can claim, with justice, that your artistry makes more demands on your intelligence, inspiration, and day's routine than does that of the painter, composer, poet. Few of the latter can work in any environment save seclusion, but the rug artist can work anywhere and remain artistic. So making hooked rugs has a distinct advantage over other artistic expressions. Noise, crowds, confusion—none of these caused you to display "artistic temperament," because they simply do not interfere with or interrupt you. Indeed, if confusion inspires a touch of jitters; if chaos, mental, physical, and emotional become too much, temporarily, no activity is quite so soothing as dropping down at the rug frame and creating a rose or a pansy. Then confusion automatically resolves itself, chaos becomes order of its own accord; nerves lose their tension, the pulse becomes normal; the day's potential hysteria has become something less than the mood inspired by the rug, and is absorbed by it.

Why hook rugs when machines do it faster, more accurately? That's exactly the reason! No machine, however exact, is ever an artist though it works out designs artists have originated. No machinery can hook mood into a rug. No machine can write "To Mother with Love" into a rug without even writing the words somewhere, as certainly as loving hands can fill a rug with love. No method of writing can be more certainly read by the loved one. People may be wary or self-conscious about expressing affection in words, but the rug done by loving hands tells much of the story without words and the rug endures much longer.

Rugs take many shapes, as corners, nooks, and crannies do. Rugs may never know the touch of a human foot, for rugs don't have to be made solely to be trodden on. They can be, literally, pictures—to hang on the wall, before the fireplace, wherever the eye of the artist sees a need. A rug can cushion the back or seat of a chair, can be a runner or fit a flight of stairs. The artist makes the decision; the result is the sum of her artistic ability. Her rugs fulfill her destiny. Few artists in other fields can claim as much; most of them strive for years for recognition while the hooker attains recognition with her very first rug.

The fame of the rugmaker may not extend as far as that of other artists, but often it extends farther; sometimes it is much more lasting. The best work of pioneer rugmakers in New England and Canada have become museum pieces, eagerly studied by rug artists of today—often freely copied because of their beauty and originality of design.

The growing ability to find something for the hooked rug in everything seen, heard, or touched is the measure of the hooked-rug artist. Many words are used here to make this clear, to inspire you to stop, look, listen, to overlook nothing that can be used—to see quickly with the artist's perceptivity items of inspiration to production that are, literally, everywhere, in everything.

Take a stroll, read a book, see a movie, attend a tea, view television, attend church, listen, talk, but above all see, and the amazing thing will not be that so much is discovered, but that so very much passed unnoticed before. All the time it was underfoot, before the eyes, entirely surrounding you, crying out to be noticed and translated into artistic expression. The world, indoors and out, is filled with dream rugs awaiting translation.

Rugmaking is an enthralling hobby. For many it is a profitable business. It can be both.

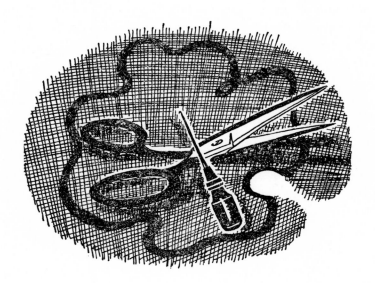

II. *Hooked-Rug Therapy*

For there is hope of a tree, if it be cut down, that it will sprout again, and that the tender branch thereof will not cease.

—Book of Job

MANY people who are frustrated, harassed, despondent, partially crippled, mentally disturbed, withdrawn, or otherwise handicapped can be helped by hooked-rug therapy. This is especially true of some veterans doomed to spend years of their lives in hospitals. I am certain of this from many personal experiences. I long ago discovered that any emotional disturbance could be allayed by sitting at my frame and doing some work on my latest rug. Often I have been asked to help old people to find themselves again in a world that seems to have passed them by, left them in corners set aside for the unwanted, but with all their faculties intact as if to make sure they suffered from neglect. I have been asked to work with shy people and have seen them take to rugmaking with delight, finding in it a way to align

12

themselves with individuals and groups from which, previously, their own shyness had excluded them. Nothing brings people together more effectively —I repeat again and again—than a commonly enjoyed hobby, of which one of the best, if not the best, is the hooking of individualistic rugs.

Grandma Moses, once known only to her neighbors, is now known to the world; she refused to stay put merely because she was getting old. She made a place for herself with her paintings; but not every woman, young or old, is a painter. Almost all women can paint with hooked rugs.

This chapter is placed early in the book with the idea of giving every woman who reads it a goal at which to aim from the moment she takes up rug hooking. There is great delight in hooking rugs, even greater satisfaction in sharing the hobby with others—as many others as possible. If they need such sharing—and every one has some secret need—the satisfaction knows virtually no bounds.

Patients in mental hospitals, old folks' homes, institutions for "other" children, veterans in hospitals throughout the nation mutely suggest work for people of vision. This is especially true of the "other" people who, for reasons that are none of the stranger's concern, are neglected by their own nearest and dearest. Women who have never known what it is to suffer with some handicapped one whom it seems impossible to help do not sit in judgment on those who know. But they can still help. There are enough women with artistic yearnings to take rug therapy to such unhappy human beings in our hospitals and institutions throughout the land; every woman who does it will enrich herself far more than she will enrich those to whom she takes the story of hooked-rug therapy. I do not suggest meddling or do-gooding, or a highly personal and obvious consciousness of being "charitable." I am sure women who share rug therapy with others will themselves receive much more from those with whom they share than they can ever transmit to them. Those women do not do the "other" people favors; they do the greatest of all favors to themselves.

Such a little initial effort is needed; just a start, an idea. The handicapped themselves, unless drowned in sloughs of despondency, find ways to express themselves that would never occur to the normal person—even the sympathetic woman. The handicapped may need no more than a few suggestions about making hooked rugs. I used the word "normal" above, meaning by it, persons who regard themselves as normal, and are so regarded by their friends, relatives, and acquaintances: but in using it I bear in mind, and suggest that readers bear in mind, that even the most nearly "normal" person is subject to emotional upsets, routine daily frustrations, worries, despair—all of which can be alleviated by some hobby such as rug hooking. How much more can this kind of "therapy" help the "other" person. By concentrating on the unfolding pattern of the rug—the lovely colors—hookers may find relaxation, and nerves lose their tension. Women who take up rug hooking as an artistic outlet, it is suggested, should begin by sharing it with those who need understanding, spiritual adjustment, personal attention, escape from innerness, aloneness. The most withdrawn man, woman, or child can be quickly induced to blossom like the most beautiful flower in his first floral design rug—and express that blossoming in the flower itself, done by his or her own hands. What could possibly induce greater satisfaction for the rug artist? Such an artist will discover that she has more grateful help than she had ever dreamed; for doctors, nurses, interns, caretakers of "homes" welcome anything that brightens the lives of their charges and that isn't bitter medicine to be taken as an act of will!

Will sharing your new hobby prove expensive? That depends entirely on your ingenuity. If you are the kind of artist whose imagination creates attractive rugs, you will accept the idea of sharing as a kind of challenge and manage it without too much extra cost—even if you have to ask others to share the "burden" that you are about to assume! If you cannot buy cloth for the shut in, you can go to the rag bag, as did your rugmaking forebears, and bundle up materials you would probably throw away, at least you can afford this lesser amount for a shut-in. You need but one cutter to cut strips for yourself and for whomever you are sharing it with. You may begin your own work first, before you discover, as I did, that sharing almost at once becomes teaching—teaching so satisfying and demanding that you scarcely have time to make your own rugs! It isn't even required that you keep ahead of your pupils once the start has been made. You are merely the inspiration, the initiator, providing the first tools, perhaps the first pattern. You should never "officiate," thus defeating your purpose. You may drop little ideas for others to pick up and hook into their rugs as if they were their very own! My experiences have shown that people who have previously been compelled by circumstances to concentrate on themselves and their personal frustrations, naturally take to rugmaking as an "escape," finding in it, after they have adjusted, that it is much more than that; it is a kind of healing.

If the housewife, the secretary, the clerk, the career woman find satisfying self-expression in hooking rugs, how much greater satisfaction will the "other" person derive if he has been on the way to giving up hope for personal im-

PHOTO BY BRUCE R. ZEISER

OLD NEW ENGLAND, *hooked by Alice Nicholson*

PHOTO BY H. LANDIS

VELVET FLOWERS, *hooked by Helen Nightengale*

PHOTO BY A. LALIME

FOREST AND GARDEN, *hooked by Eva MacCrae*

PHOTO BY A. LALIME

FLOWER BELLS, *hooked by Mildred Smith*

ELEPHANT EARS, *hooked by Ora Andersen*

MELODY, *hooked by Madaline Peach*

AMBER GRAIN, *hooked by Celia Flynn*

NEW HAMPSHIRE ANTIQUE, *hooked by Mildred Smith*

APRIL, *hooked by Mildred Smith*

PHOTO BY A. LALIME

FLIP AND FLOP, *hooked by Elizabeth McManus*

PHOTO BY A. LALIME

EARLY THRESHOLD, *hooked by Alice Nicholson*

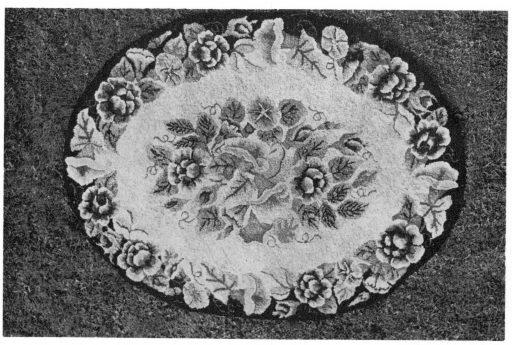

CENTURY-OLD AFGHAN, *hooked by Mary Healey*

PHOTO BY A. LALIME

OYSTER BAY ANTIQUE, *hooked by Elizabeth Hetherington*

PHOTO BY A. LALIME

PEEKING PANSIES, *hooked by Celia Flynn*

POPPY SEED, *hooked by Viola Spousta*

OCEAN SWELL, *hooked by Billie Rometti*

PHOTO BY A. LALIME

PROVINCIAL, *hooked by Elizabeth McManus*

ROSE OF SHARON, *hooked by Florence L. McLean*

RUFFLES, *hooked by Lena Nichols*

PHOTO BY A. LALIME

CLEMATIS, *hooked by Barbara Horton*

PHOTO BY A. LALIME

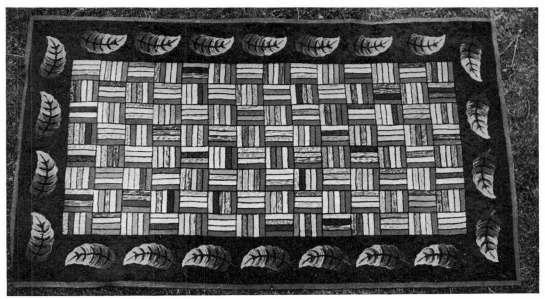

CHESTNUT LEAF BORDER, *hooked by Mildred Smith*

PHOTO BY A. LALIME

PHOTO BY A. LALIME

BLOCK PRINTS, *hooked by Effie Gordon*

MR. AND MRS. CURRIER, *hooked by Mildred Smith*

HOME FOR THANKSGIVING, *hooked by Mildred Smith*

HALLELUJAH, *hooked by Pearl Penley*

IRIS, *hooked by Mildred Smith*

FLOWER MEDLEY, *hooked by Billie Rometti*

FRUIT MEDLEY, *hooked by Claire Heffron*

WIDE ORIENTAL, *hooked by Mildred Smith*

PLUME LEAF RUNNER, *hooked by Mildred Smith*

PUNGENT PINE, *hooked by Mildred Smith*

ACANTHUS OVAL, *hooked by Gertrude Brendle*

CHATTERBOX, *hooked by Mrs. George Denison*

SHERATON, *hooked by Mrs. Luther Moyer*

MANDALAY, *hooked by Maude Greene*

WHITE OAK, *hooked by Helen Conkey*

PETERBOROUGH ANTIQUE, *hooked by Mary Mott*

PLUMES, *hooked by Alice Nicholson*

PAISLEY SHAWL, *hooked by Louise Hunter Zeiser*

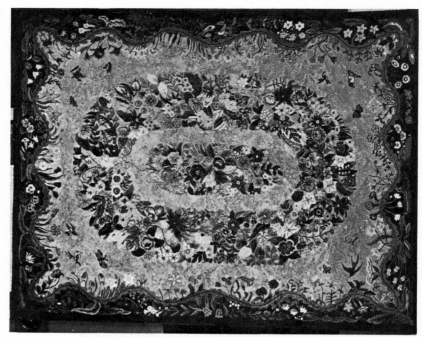

MILLE FLEURS, *hooked by Evelyn Drummond*

PHOTO BY GUNNING

WILDWOOD, *hooked by Frances Wiggin*

PHOTO BY GUNNING

THANKSGIVING, *hooked by Dot Mattlin*

NATIONAL BOUQUET, *hooked by Frances Wiggin*

LILY POOL, *hooked by Bertha Bainton*

JOAN OF ARC, *hooked by Inez Hartley*

ROUMANIAN CONVENT, *hooked by Louise Hunter Zeiser*

RIVIERA, *hooked by Louise Hunter Zeiser*

VERBENAS, *hooked by Louise Hunter Zeiser*

PASTEL, *hooked by Ann Borodell Denison*

NATURE'S PETS, *hooked by Eileen Lewis*

ARIEL, *hooked by Iris Guertin*

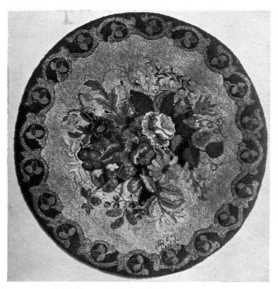

QUEENSLAND, *hooked by Alice Rogler*

OH! SUSANNAH, *hooked by Barbara Dawson*

SUNBURST, *hooked by Louise Hunter Zeiser*

FIREFLY, *hooked by Helen Page*

TRIPLE SCALLOPED FEATHERS, *hooked by Louise Hunter Zeiser*

35" x 120" — $13.00

U.S.A. WELCOME   *Hooked by Louise Hunter Zeiser*   NAVY WELCOME

DOUBLE PANEL CENTER, *hooked by Maud Eshelman*   PHOTO BY LANDIS

#520 A 27" x 90 — $8.00
#520 B 27" x 132 — $11.50
(Triple Panel).

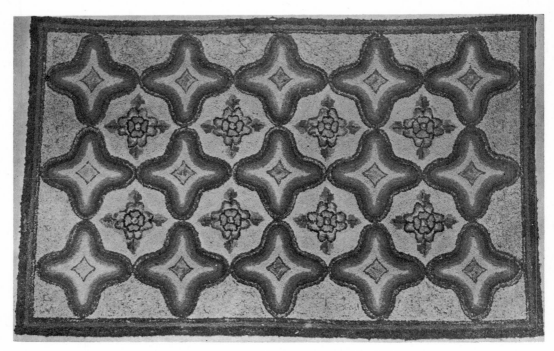

QUEEN ANNE, *hooked by Louise Hunter Zeiser*

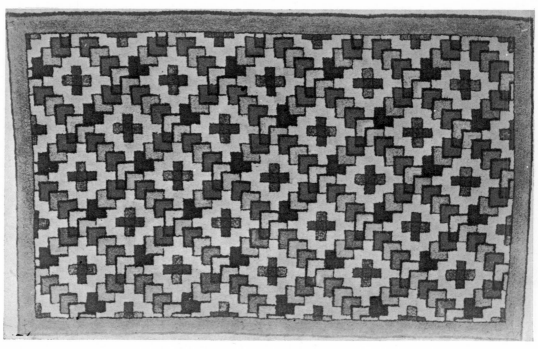

STEPPED MEDALLIONS, *hooked by Louise Hunter Zeiser*

ROSE OF CHINA, *hooked by Louise Hunter Zeiser*

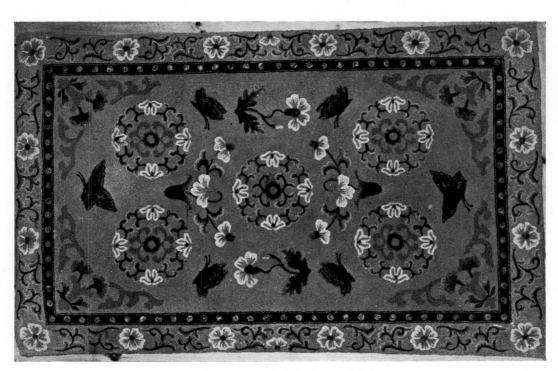

PEKING, *hooked by Emily Finlay*

667.

45" x 72" - $9.00

TEA FOR TWO, *hooked by Mrs. Edward Young*

SPRING SERENADE, *hooked by Mary Clarke*

JEWEL BOX, *hooked by Emily Finlay*

FOUR DOZEN ROSES, *hooked by Emily Finlay*

MARIGOLD HEROIC, *hooked by Louise Hunter Zeiser*

HORN OF PLENTY HEROIC, *hooked by Louise Hunter Zeiser*

provement! It is a sure way of throwing out a lifeline. For one thing, rug-making does something for the personality no doctor, nurse, or surgeon has ever been able to do—diverts his attention from himself and his frustrations, frustrations often close to the point of explosion. Rugmaking requires attention, and not even the most self-conscious handicapped person can concentrate on himself and hook a rug simultaneously. A few persons will be found, of course, who prefer to concentrate on themselves, who "enjoy poor health," and these are difficult to reach.

You who share will find that you have provided yourself with a potential storehouse of ideas—color combinations, dyeing techniques, and other riches of the spirit of which you never dreamed. By opening doors, or channels, for others, you open new doors and channels for yourself as your storehouse of rug experience is given to others, all of their ideas automatically swing open for you. Fascinating?

It is much more than that! It is thoroughly rewarding. In this task of sharing, as nowhere else, bread cast upon waters returns multiplied. Examine this statement carefully, for in it lies the proof that hooking rugs is an artistic expression; it isn't a question of taking artistic expression on faith, but of seeing it in actual operation! Read proof in results.

I came to Pennsylvania with ideas about hooking rugs. Not finding any artistic rugs being hooked and so many new friends who desired to learn, almost against my will I became a teacher. Put on my mettle I had to prove what I could do. As I taught, my pupils gave me their ideas freely, frankly, in perfect friendliness. I learned more while teaching than I could have learned alone. I have been learning and growing spiritually ever since. I have pupils beyond my personal capacity—one of the principal reasons for this book, each copy of which may inspire some new teacher I may never meet, though I'd like to, to help reach many of those who desire to learn.

A small business is the dream of the handicapped veteran, so that he will have to ask neither odds nor help from anyone. His wants are simpler than those of men who circulate in the world and feel that they are busy. And, again, how about the old folks in homes who, if not there because they themselves down the years have saved up nest eggs against just such a contingency, must depend on loved ones for "extras"? The rug artist can easily imagine, long before she herself becomes old and withdraws from life, how welcome old people will find any channel by which their aged hands can produce a few pennies that are their very own! As long as the hands work and the eyes can see, the old may be proudly independent, at least in the "extras" department—though most old folks will take their small money and buy presents for the very people they feel regard them as burdens!

Rugmaking is not like reading, to the shut-in, or like playing cards, or singing—for it remains. Frames, cloth, dyes, crochet hooks, clippers, scissors, are material; they don't vanish into thin air to be seen and heard no more. The shut-in can use them until they fall apart; they can use them any hour of the day or night, and anywhere. Rugs are something that can be seen, handled, absorbed.

Share your scrapbooks containing color pictures of advertisements for china, curtains, linoleum, furniture, glass, even though they having nothing to do directly with rugmaking; if they are done in lovely colors they become grist to the mill of the hooker, who is always searching for the striking color and color combination. Color is the blood stream of hooked rugs and men who have had quite too much time to think can be relied upon to exploit all possible sources of color schemes; so can the old, the shy, the withdrawn. Start them and keep them going until they are on the way; then they will share with the teacher.

It must be obvious at this point that rug therapy is not just for the handi-capped, the mentally deficient, the despondent, the bored. It is literally for everyone who has stepped on a hooked rug and been conscious of it; it's more so for anyone watching a rug being hooked; it's complete therapy of great value, for whoever, of either sex, of whatever age, actually begins to hook rugs.

Self-expression!

If the self is expressed, how can the self have time to worry, fret, despair? There is neither time, opportunity, nor place—if the rug-hooking frame, with growing rug attached, occupies the foreground!

> No one could tell me where my soul might be;
> I searched for God and he eluded me;
> I sought my brother out and found all three.
> —ERNEST H. CROSBY

III. *Equipment Needs*

I have found that all people dull in conversation
and hateful to look at are those who have no hobbies.

—Yüan Chunglang

SIMPLE inexpensive equipment is the first need of the hooker. Of the equipment listed below the first four are *musts;* the remainder may be procured as you see a need for it.

1. A solid, well-built, adjustable easel-type frame.
2. A small, fine hook set in a small wooden handle.
3. A pattern stamped on good quality India burlap.
4. Woolen materials, of all kinds (do not use mixtures of cotton, silk, rayon, or even worsteds).

5. A cutting machine, the Rigby model, which is a favorite.
6. A pair of hooking scissors.
7. A rug-lite, a blue bulb for nightwork.
8. Hard pastel crayons.
9. Dyes, Cushing's Perfection Dyes recommended.
10. Colored swatches such as the Rockwell Studios offer.
11. Shoelaces or old silk stockings to tie the pattern tight to the sidebars.
12. Bank pins recommended to take up slack in pattern.
13. Pluckers (eyebrow tweezers for ripping).
14. Scrapbook.

Material from which we derive inspiration that may be kept in the scrapbook.

    a. Pictures of colored flowers, from seed catalogues and from magazines.
    b. Wallpaper samples (floral, leaf, and scroll designs).
    c. Small cretonne samples of floral and scroll designs.
    d. Small samples of drapery materials, floral patterns, and scrolls.
    e. Floral greeting cards.
    f. Scenic greeting cards (especially winter and farm scenes for Currier and Ives's rug patterns).
    g. Color advertising in magazines.
    h. Interior decorating pictures.
    i. Pressed flowers.
    j. Floral prints (paintings and pictures from magazines).
    k. Samples of plaid material.
    l. Floral and fruit designs on some of the plastic materials.
    m. Floral and fruit designs on plastic place mats.
    n. A collection of old German needlepoint patterns in color.
    o. Colored pictures of cross-stitch patterns.

Sources of Inspiration:
    a. Visiting hooked-rug exhibits.
    b. Study Oriental and broadloom rug patterns.
    c. Study old hooked rugs in museums.
    d. Real flowers.

Among the items of equipment listed above the frame is one of the most important. Some rug artists work without a frame but I have never been able to do this and do not recommend it. It is better to be comfortable. The frame makes the work easier, faster, more enjoyable. I prefer a sturdy,

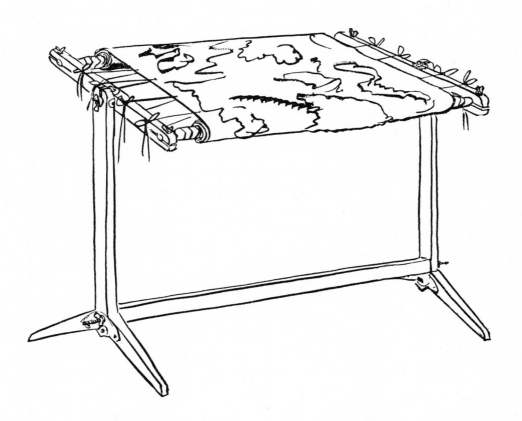

well-built, adjustable frame of the easel type. It can be tilted to suit anyone. It should be of just the right height for you to work on it easily from a straight-back chair, as easily as you sit at your writing desk. Old style frames, without rollers, or anything other than the easel type frame, should not be used to start a lifetime hobby. Nothing is quite so exasperating to a teacher or pupil as a frame that collapses at surprising intervals or one that is not made for hooking.

Given the proper frame, with the burlap pattern drawn tightly as required, you can sit before the frame with a relaxed mind and body; the fingers glide across the pattern without strain. The burlap should be affixed sufficiently taut that a ball can almost be bounced upon it. A taut pattern makes hooking easier, faster, and the loops are naturally and more easily aligned. Any slack in the burlap makes the work harder, tends to make the loops uneven. A better product will result if each step is taken in proper sequence; if none of the little things are overlooked; the work itself will be more enjoyable.

The second requirement is the hook. A fine hook is required for fine detail work with closely woven burlap and thinly cut strips of wool. I like crochet hooks because I like the smooth steel and the smoothly rounded end of the hook. You may buy such a hook, have a few inches of the end opposite the hook cut off, then procure a wooden handle that has already been holed at a hardware store. Affixing the cut end of the crochet hook into the hole in the wooden handle is a simple operation. It should, of course, be fastened firmly so it won't loosen. This kind of hook will cost perhaps twenty-five cents, or a ready-made hook will cost seventy-five cents to a dollar. Many department stores have hooks that are somewhat similar, but the handles are too large for the average woman's hand, while the shank is too large and too coarse. Fine work requires a fine hook with a small handle that is comfortable in the hand. Handle and hook together should be about four inches in length. (See sketch.)

Number three on the list is the pattern, which calls for the exercise of artistic choice. I recommend Mrs. Zeiser's Heirloom patterns * that are printed on a good grade of finely woven India burlap. This makes it possible to work with very fine strips, hooked through almost every burlap mesh. Burlap patterns may be procured from several sources. I especially like the Heirloom patterns because I find them so inspiring. They are always the patterns I wish I had evolved myself. Thanks to beautiful designs like Mrs. Zeiser's, the hand-made rug, after years of eclipse in competition with the machine, is again coming into its own. Rug artists with a natural flair for design will quickly

* See page 104.

evolve their own and are encouraged to do so. However, with so many beautiful designs in every size from which to choose it seems foolish for anyone who finds designing difficult to compete with the rug designer.

A cutting machine is not absolutely necessary, but evenly cut strips vastly improve the hooked rug. A cutter cuts the cloth to an exact width, saving hours of work that would be required if done by hand. Not only does a cutter save time, but even strips make hooking easier, more enjoyable. The Rigby is a fine cutting machine—a good investment, in my opinion. Blades of many sizes are procurable for the Rigby; all are easily attached.

Hooking scissors are not absolutely necessary, either, but they make hooking easier, more comfortable, and are therefore worth consideration by the busy housewife. The rugger who has a pair would not be without them. The bent handles of the scissors, allowing the operator to cut horizontally without touching the rug with her knuckles, enables her to cut the ends drawn through the right, or top, side of the rug, without cutting the loops. Regular scissors can be used, but it is more difficult to cut horizontally with them. It is sometimes difficult to get hooking scissors. Wiss used to make them, but Wiss hooking scissors at the moment of writing are not, to my knowledge, available, though hooking scissors of other makes are carried by some department stores. Make sure, however, of the quality of hooking scissors of any unknown trademark before you buy. (See sketch.)

Selection of material is a very important step. Many housewives, since traditionally they have done so, look to their rag bags for their rugs—for cloth that has served every other conceivable purpose. The rugger who is essentially an artist plans to put the best of herself into her rugs. She knows that hand-hooked rugs are potential heirlooms and merit the finest in materials. Into her rugs go love, labor, hours of work so that rugs are made to deserve more than the worn-out materials of the rag bag. In New England there are many places where new material consisting of mill ends, remnants, or mat rags—the term a mill gives to ends that are usually sold to paper mills as scrap—may be obtained. These places buy up all such scrap, all manufacturers' clippings, and these are fine for hooking materials. A number of places where such cloth may be obtained will be given in this book. Desirable materials are often most difficult to obtain through the mail. New Englanders are more fortunate than most, for in any direction, within reasonable driving distance, they can reach mills, warehouses, or stores that cater directly to the rugmaking public.

Gabardine and serge, which are worsteds, are tightly woven and have a hard finish; such material makes it more suitable for men's wear, but does not lend itself to hooking as well as woolens. Materials such as flannels and tweeds and many plaids hook easier, and each loop through blends into others, giving a rich, soft effect. Worsteds and tightly woven materials show every separate loop hooked, standing virtually alone, crude, lacking in beauty. Wool outwears other materials, and is easier to clean. Many beautiful effects are worked out with plaids and tweeds, which add character to the rug. Very heavy and firmly woven materials should be cut with a #3 cutter or $\frac{3}{32}''$ (Rigby sizes); the same for materials of a very heavy pile. Average weight woolens call for the #4 or $\frac{1}{8}''$ cutter that produces strips an eighth of an inch wide. The #5 or $\frac{5}{32}''$ cutter should be used for materials that are thin or light-weight. Your strips may be of any length from about three to ten inches. Longer strips are used for backgrounds and borders.

All weights of woolens except very heavy blanket material or men's heavy woolen sport coats or jackets can be used; but never combine wool with silk, cotton, rayon, or nylon. Woolen garments that still have some obvious value should not be thrown away. Skirts that someone may have outgrown may still fit neatly into that new rug.

A rug-lite is helpful for nightwork, some teachers recommending a blue bulb. A good light is required for working with delicate shades and colors. The rug-lite attaches to the frame and can be adjusted to the exact spot where you are hooking.

As for the hard pastel crayons, they are of especial value to the teacher of rugmaking. They are not necessary to the beginner, but to the teacher, and to the pupil who hooks by herself, a few hard pastel crayons help to visualize the colors and shades planned for the rug; they provide you with a kind of preview of the finished rug. A teacher finds crayons helpful in planning each rug in a class, which in turn helps the pupil remember what a teacher has planned, in color, for each design, each flower. Rug artists dream out their rugs; crayons help them to keep their dreams in mind. They are a way of keeping notes.

There are several sources from which colored swatches especially dyed for making flowers, leaves, and scrolls may be purchased. These are a boon to the novice who begins with little and has a natural fear of trying something new, like dyeing, before she has become adept at the new hobby of hooking rugs. Colored swatches are valuable to teacher and pupil alike. To a teacher who is handicapped for materials and is starting a new class, colored swatches are of immense value. She can work out shadings for her new pupils with five color gradations that help to teach the novice that instead of the six rainbow colors there are hundreds of shades and tints of every color. The Rockwell Studios offer a very good selection of colored swatches of 100 per cent wool cloth that may be cut into very fine strips for hooking.

Cushing Perfection Dyes are my choice for fast colors. Cushing also provides a vast variety of colors of good quality and fast dye from which to choose. (See chapter on dyeing.)

The collection of inspirational material begins with the first rug, continues as long as you live. The material from which you build is so much part of yourself that it is almost presumptuous to offer suggestions. But if you are a novice you may not know exactly how to begin, so it is with this fact in mind, and somewhat apologetically, that the author offers a few suggestions.

When I came to Pennsylvania I was suddenly on my own. Before leaving Massachusetts I had always had a teacher upon whom to lean, and a good one, as well as friends who assembled to discuss rugs, and hook for an afternoon. Before I could catch my breath I found myself teaching hooked rug-making! I turned to every available source for help and am now turning over such inspirational material to those who may be beginners. There is no such thing as too much help.

I realized the paramount importance of planning the colors of a rug. I sought color combinations and schemes from every conceivable source. The attention of all would-be ruggers is directed, in this connection, to colored advertisements in many magazines. Every detail of even the poorest of them —and very few poor ones see publication!—is carefully thought out, even though details in themselves may have nothing to do with the articles the advertisements purport to sell. There is such keen competition in industry that most big business houses employ a staff of well-trained and well-equipped artists and designers. These artists plan colored advertisements in magazines to catch the eye. Sometimes it seems impossible to believe that such exquisitely executed pictures are advertisements. I recently noted a striking picture that carried no legend of any kind, but the mere fact of finding no explanation sent me scurrying through the magazine for an explanation—which perhaps was what the artist planned in the first place.

Because artists of today go to so much effort to work out every little detail of color, striving always for that harmony that is also the goal of the hook-rugger, much may be found in magazines that will exactly fit the color scheme of the planned rug, a rug planned to fit the color scheme of a given room.

Examples: China, glass, furniture, wall covering, paint, carpeting, lamps, curtains—all are products nationally advertised. Obviously many of them have nothing directly to do with rugs, unless they are part of the furnishings of the room for which the rug is intended. But the artist who planned the color scheme for the advertisements automatically provides you with ideas for color schemes that you may work into your patterns. One color advertisement in my collection was planned by an artist for a stocking manufacturer. The picture shows a model dressed in a beautiful red purple dress on which the lights play, producing highlights and depths of color; deep blue purple and light orchid violets form the bouquet for the front of the dress. The background is green where the light strikes; the green is a lovely chartreuse that blends into a deeper yellow green, shading into a bronze green, then into a blue green. These colors could be worked into a rug, while the touch of a neutral shade for the nylon stockings suggests the perfect background upon which to hook the rug. The artist added a touch of bittersweet in the background for accent. I never would have thought of combining that color with the others, yet there it was proved to be harmonious. The advertisement is rich in color and will certainly lose nothing when transmuted into the hooked rug—unless the artist loses something somewhere! What more could even the alchemist desire?

I like to collect colored pictures of flowers from magazines and from seed catalogues. I find that such pictures help me to determine the color values of certain flowers but do not help to work out the shadings in hooking those same flowers. The colors are but the beginning, the suggestion. Even here you must not lean; you must create, improvise. I do think that you will get more help from paintings of flowers, for the artist who paints must also use highlights and shadows; she must use shading effects to separate petals and to give perspective. I recently came across the *National Geographic Magazine* for July, 1947, that contained paintings of over one hundred flowers by the artist Else Bostelman. Such pictures are wonderful to keep in your scrapbook for they will give you many ideas to use in shading your flowers for that new rug pattern.

You may find that wallpaper, with its many floral designs and scrolls, often with some truly enthralling shadings, a great help and a guidepost to planning a rug. Many patterns may also have a complete color scheme already worked out for you.

Needlepoint furnishes wonderful ideas for shading flowers and leaves and so may be a guide to mastering shading, as well as planning colors for certain leaves and flowers. If you do not have any needlepoint in your home, maybe your friends will gladly permit you to copy ideas from their needlepoint pieces.

Whenever you have the opportunity, notice floral designs on china and lamp shades. I have a set of plates that has offered some helpful ideas, i.e., on the outside border of the plate is a gold scroll design on a robin's egg blue background, the floral center is painted on a cream background. There is a lovely deep rose-to-white tulip, a deep purple dahlia, a few small flowers in white, pink, blue, and yellow. The leaves are blue green and bronze-to-gold. This particular color scheme could easily be transferred to a rug design.

Also for my scrapbook I add interior decorating pictures that are done in color. Being a teacher I collect, of course, not only the color schemes I like but as many different ones as I can find. Then I add samples of cretonne and drapery materials, which provide hints on the shading of flowers to the persistent hunter for variety in color, tints, hues—in short, in the limitless realm of color.

Many samples of plaid materials also go into my scrapbook because I have found them to be, literally, indexes to the planning of color schemes for many rugs. Every plaid has been planned by an artist, therefore it is, in itself, a color scheme. Many plaids have a predominant color; so have many rugs. The parallel is inescapable. You simply extend and expand the plan of the artist in plaid, attaining a result, in a rug, of which the artist surely never dreamed. I have one piece of plaid, for example, that contains green, brown, yellow, red, rust, bittersweet, eggshell—all blended and complemented in accordance with the plan of the artist who conceived that particular plaid. Use this as a basis for a color scheme in a rug as follows: brown for the outside background, green for the scroll and leaves, yellow or rust veining in the scroll and leaves, many shades of yellow, red, rust, gold, bittersweet, brown, and tan for the flowers. They will blend in the rug as beautifully as I can see they do in the plaid. In effect I merely "stretch" the plaid into a rug.

The collection of wool is of primary importance. You will discover, as every hooker does, that with ten shades of green you still may not have the right shade to suit the teacher! So the accumulation of wool begins and grows to such proportions that you may find as I did that not only the cellar and the attic and spare room were filled with boxes of wool, but gradually the closets and drawers were being packed with wool. I guess my husband patiently put up with this accumulation of wool as long as he could. Then one day he drove a truck up to the door and unloaded a huge box that he said would contain my rags from now on. My father, who had been an undertaker in a small town in Massachusetts, had kept several large boxes, which caskets come in, in his barn. These boxes he had partitioned off into sections and lined with tar paper (an excellent way of keeping moths out of your wools; I've tried it for ten years and it works). Dad had for a number of years used those boxes to store buffalo robes. So the "box" went into my cellar and into it went my rug rags. It was welcome, for no longer did wool rags hit us in the face when we opened a closet door. But when I came to move to Pennsylvania the movers took one look and said, "Don't tell us that thing is going!" I replied that the truck would not leave without it—nor I. Puzzled, they asked what it contained, and when I replied "rags" they made me open it and prove it to them. They only shook their heads and loaded it on the truck, but by the disgusted looks they gave me I can guess that they said to themselves, "Women!"

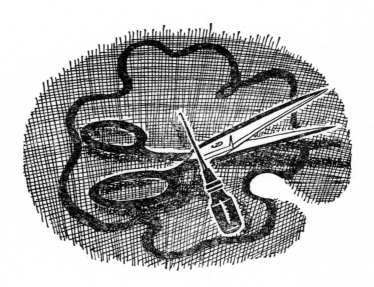

IV. *Selection of Design*

The acquiring of culture is the developing
of an avid hunger for knowledge and beauty.

—JESSE LEE BENNETT

A TEACHER finds pupils every bit as interesting, and diverse, as hooked-rug designs. Why, for example, did a certain design please one pupil and not another? Simply because no two people are alike; each is a self, an individual, seeking self-expression. No real teacher will seek to impress herself too strongly upon her pupils because she knows that pupils who graduate from her class as pale copies of the teacher are not artists at all. On what should you base your choice of design? Some teachers say that you should choose a pattern to fit a room, or a place, or a niche. I personally do not hold rigidly to this idea. I treat it at some length in this book in order not to impose my own ideas but to make them available as springboards of the pupils' own. I think a pattern should also be chosen to fit a person, a personality.

Geometric and Orientals are usually considered for dens or men's bed-rooms, nursery scenes for children's rooms, floral patterns for women's bed-rooms, etc.; but some women choose a design because its lines appeal or because the finished rug of the same design has been seen at some exhibit or in some friend's possession. My personal selections are based solely on designs I feel I must develop. Hooking rugs is my hobby; I love it; but if a pattern appeals to me I develop it whether or not it fits any room I know of. Some day I may have a use for it; if not it will make a fine gift. I need many rugs of many sizes but I do not create patterns, or choose certain patterns because I need a certain size or design for a certain room. I pick a design I know I will enjoy hooking. My husband expressed a desire for a certain design so I hooked it for him. The pattern is an odd size, fitting no place exactly or artistically, but we use it just the same and like it.

I have a friend who hooks only Oriental patterns. She is a lover of flowers and probably feels that even the flowers in some of the older designs are not artistic enough. There is also the hint that she loves flowers so much she cannot endure to hook them into rugs to be stepped on.

A pattern is chosen then because it appeals or because the size is right for a certain spot in a certain room, or because the type of design goes with the furnishings in a room. Whatever the reason for your choice it should be your own. No instructions to any artist can be exact, simply because no two artists would decorate their homes in the same way.

Some pupils go to rug-hooking class knowing exactly what they want in design, size, and color. Others who doubt their own ability deliberate over size and amount of detail work in a pattern, usually deciding on something that will not be too much work! This is all right for the novice, but after a start has been made, why not try to accomplish larger and more difficult rugs? If you are a novice and contemplate a piece of burlap on which a design has been stamped you may find it difficult to visualize the completed rug and to comprehend the potentialities of color. At first the artist in you may be asleep, or dozing; to some, such imaginations may always be a problem that will have to be solved in detail in accordance with your natural ability to visualize. Others use trial and error until real creative ability seems more or less to mold itself into a thing of personal joy and satisfaction.

I study each new pattern produced by Mrs. Zeiser. If it appeals to me I dream over its color possibilities, planning its details as I lie awake at night or while I wash clothes or clean the house. Often in the midst of some house-hold chore I drop whatever I am doing, take up the pattern, spread it on the floor and color in some ideas. Planning is a real joy that has in it great possibilities for personal development. To teach hooking is to enjoy this art at its fullest. Watching others develop creative ability under one's instruction and supervision is the teacher's richest experience.

A teacher must project herself into every rug she works on for others. She must forget her own likes and dislikes if she is to be a good teacher. This is somewhat difficult to do both in design and color. One noted teacher consistently refuses to work up color for pupils—except in the pastels. Now, all ruggers may like pastel colors to some extent, but few wish to concentrate on rugs exclusively of these light tones.

Sometimes women ask me for help in planning rugs designed by themselves or copied from other crudely designed patterns done by persons obviously not designers or artists. This is a waste of time for the would-be designer and the teacher. Unless you have real talent for design why should you attempt two arts, when so many beautiful designs, drawn by artists, are available? A beautiful design may be spoiled by poor workmanship or color, but it is impossible to beautify a poorly designed pattern. Women like Mrs. Zeiser evolve such inspirational patterns that it is a waste of time for you to attempt design. And the beautiful design, I am glad to repeat, which is spoiled by poor workmanship, is never lost. The poor workman can rip it out and do it over, better. Save the time that might be lost hunting out design; use it in hooking beautiful designs already available. I am not personally interested in creating design. I find inspiration in the skeletal designs provided by artists of design. I can seldom contain myself until I have started to match whatever skill I may possess as a hooker with the already demonstrated skill of the designer. The ardent hooker finds joy in wool and burlap, especially if the burlap is overlaid with an irresistible design. It is easy to see, with a little practice, what the designer had in mind; the challenge to the hooker is to come up to the designer's expectations, though the designer may never see the finished rug.

Before copying the patterns of early American rugs, you should bear in mind that the rugmakers of a few decades ago had none of the facilities that every rugmaker has today. To copy something old, generally speaking, is to insist on standing still, for the pioneers of rugmaking were distinguished more by what they lacked, and what they made of it, than by their art as rugmakers. A few, a very few, of our early American rugs, are priceless, preserved in some of our New England museums. Many thousands are crude, preserved only because they are old. Pioneer women had no designs from which to copy, no books, none of the vast selective choice today's women have, so that even potentially real artists were dreadfully handicapped. Some women of pioneer days appear to have had little or no artistic ability, yet they made rugs. Some women had considerable ability but they lacked materials. Some few were unquestionably artists as proved by their surviving work. They did their own designing because there were no commercial designs, and some of these indicate great talent.

The rug artist of today will understand why the pioneers kept at it; like the women of today, they must express themselves. Rugs could be just rugs, to keep the feet warm in winter, but few women settled simply for utility. Almost all of them had the urge to beauty; they left inspiration for the vast majority of today's ruggers.

As a home-economics graduate I have studied many types of handwork, needle- and craftwork. They appeal to me greatly. I am not a perfectionist, but as a child, and later in college, I learned that if something didn't come out right it should be ripped out and done over. The end justifies the reworking. The greatest rug artist continues to learn. When she ceases to learn she is no longer an artist.

I admire the work of any artist in any field, in weaving, in ceramics, painting, leather, wood, silver, block printing—anything born of the imagination, requiring skill of hands, heart, and brain. I have some needlework done by an ancestor. To me it is priceless; represents hours of work and was, I am sure, executed with the patience of the true craftsman; is beautiful in design and coloring—proof that the designer and executrix was an artist of great skill in needlepoint, petit point, and beadwork. I cannot match her skill. I am sure few of us today could or would spend the hours so patiently over such fine work.

We of today have come a long way in the art of hooking rugs. I don't believe in standing still, even on rugs. In a world that advances on all fronts it is enough that the homemaker still produces beauty with her hands! It is better to keep moving with the times, making progress with your contemporaries. Just because many of our ancestors made rugs from old rags and old burlap bags and crude designs is no reason we should continue.

Some teachers, strangely, do not approve of design that calls for realistic flowers. I have never understood this stand, for the would-be artist in rugs finds much joy in flowers that seem to come to life. Every petal should curl; the way a rose, jonquil, poppy, or lily bows its head should be so true to life that you hesitate to step on the finished rug lest you hurt the flowers. Such rugs can be used as wall hangings, beyond the touch of rude feet, where the rugger can have her beauty and keep it, too!

Nature is filled with beauty beyond the power of the greatest artists to improve and the artistic urge is to copy it with loving fidelity, even if the result is so real that one cringes every time a heavy foot steps on the rug without apologizing. The joy of being able to create a realistic flower outweighs, for the novice, all the cringes; rather, the would-be artist can endure the cringes better than she can endure life without the chance to create such beauty. If you cannot bear to hook realistic flowers, you should still retain enough personal independence to strive for the ultimate beauty no matter who walks roughshod over your rugs!

Beautiful, lovely, realistic flower designs in needlepoint are often used as chair seats adapted to any posterior! Take note of facts with a smile, however wry, and refuse to be detoured into any artistic dead ends.

Realistic designs are a joy to bring to life in wool. They make it easier for the artist to paint with wool. The older type of designs often have flowers that are difficult to distinguish, impossible to classify, flowers of fantasy. These flowers cannot be brought to life, for if you wonder what they are when you begin you still wonder when you have finished with them. The result is a vague emptiness where there should have been personal satisfaction.

Each generation of rug artists should develop its rugs in designs and workmanship to the best of its ability. If the succeeding generation does not better its work that generation fails, or the previous generation was ahead of its time. The best of the previous generation should be used, of course, as a basis on which to build—not as a fading laurel on which to stand. At the same time, since it must be obvious to you that the very best you produce will pass away, you should strive to make it so outstanding that it will last longer and be more beautiful than any you have hitherto made.

I believe it is best not to concentrate on Orientals or florals, or else you limit yourself as a rugmaker. Enjoy all designs, thereby increasing your knowledge and skill as a rug artist.

V. Preparation of Rug Frame
and Pattern

Beauty will mold each thought that lives with me—
I shall remember only lovely things.

—WILLA HOEY

THE poles, or rollers, to which the rug is attached to be hooked, must
be bound or "bandaged." It is the simplest and best way to fasten the
rug to the frame. The rollers parallel each other, their ends fit into
round holes in the ends of the frame arms, which are equipped with set-
screws that can be run down to hold the rollers firmly wherever desired. The
poles, or rollers, can be seen in the accompanying sketch. Binding the rollers

32

is important for two reasons: (1) you must fasten the rug to the poles in some manner and the binding is permanent and ready for each succeeding rug. Strong material should be chosen, (2) if hooking a square or rectangular rug you should be able to hook to the edge of the pattern. In order to do this the burlap must be sewed to the "bandage" on the poles, sewing through one thread of the burlap as indicated in the sketch.

Start with the bandage or binding of the rollers. A four-inch strip of cloth, four times as long as the roller to be bound, should be folded lengthwise in the middle and the end of material thumbtacked to the edge of the top of the roller. Then the material is wound spirally around the roller, covering the preceding raw edge with each spiral for its entire length, thumbtacking again at the other end of the pole. It is best if the strips are sewed together on the bias, making a continuous strip of material to wind. It is less likely to loosen or unwind when the rug is sewed to it.

Now the pattern. If you are making a rectangular or square rug, the following procedure is best. (See sketch on page 34.) Hooking through one inch double thickness produces a better finished edge and longer wearing rug.

The burlap should not be cut until it is ready to sew! This is most important, since the burlap frays so easily. Most patterns provide several extra inches of burlap that must be cut off. Before cutting away this extra burlap, measure one inch beyond outside line of pattern, then cut away remainder of burlap. Now this one inch of burlap beyond edge is folded under the pattern, on wrong side, and hemmed to it. This double edge is hooked along with the rest of the pattern. But at the corners this one inch folded down would produce four thicknesses of material. It is almost impossible to hook through this, so the corners are mitered as follows: (See sketch on page 34.)

At corners we measure in one and one-half inches from the edge and cut out a bit of burlap in the shape of an L, the cutout being rectangular in shape. If cut is made too close to the folds or the two cut edges come together, the burlap cannot be secured; it will fray easily and the hooking will not hold. Nor does the cut extend closer to the fold than one quarter of an inch. The rug is now hemmed around the edges, mitered corners included. The rug is then ready to attach to the end poles, or rollers.

The folded edge of the rug is sewed to the edge of the poles, with a small close overhand stitch, with heavy button thread. The stitch is made through only one thread of the burlap, the stitching VERY CLOSE. This is done so that when the pattern is pulled taut the stitches will not pull the burlap apart. This also makes hooking possible to the extreme edge of the rug's pat-

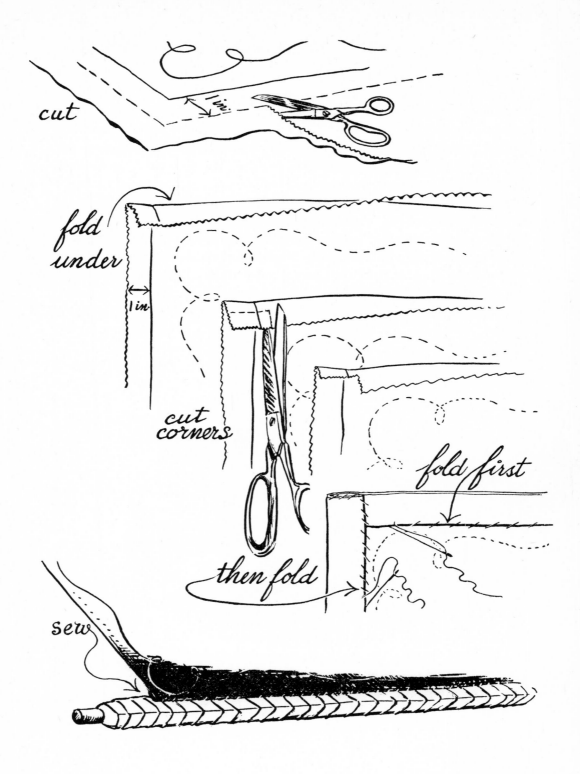

cut

fold
under

1 in

cut
corners

fold first

then fold

sew

tern; when the rug is done all that remains is to snip the stitching. If burlap shows, you can whip the edge with background color of wool yarn, or when hooking, the last two rows may be hooked higher. You may also touch up burlap with dye.

It is best to bind the oval or round rug with rug binding. It can be purchased at department stores and notion counters. No extra burlap is cut away from the oval or round rug—or *half*-round rug—until the hooked rug is finished. Stitch the binding to the burlap. The edge of rug binding is stitched to the outer edge of rug, marking the finished edge of the round, half-round, or oval rug's pattern. The other edge of binding is held down by a basting thread to the opposite side of burlap beyond the printed pattern.

When the rug is finished the basting thread is removed from the rug binding. The extra burlap is cut away, leaving one half to three quarters of an inch of burlap under the rug binding. You then hem the binding to underside of rug.

VI. A *Study In Color*

Colors brilliant and dull pass before us and we care not; but a painter brushes them upon a canvas and reveals to us the hidden glories.

—ROBERT WESTON

TO WOMEN everywhere color is a magic word; it suggests all sorts of exciting possibilities. It has been said that "color goes on forever; it is eternal, divine."

By your choice of color you reflect your personality. Your clothes, the furnishings of your home, or flowers in your garden, all mirror you who chose them. Everyone likes color and most of us hunger for a certain color. They say your personality traits can be read by your favorite color—but that is another story.

Color and color combinations are not only interesting to most people but also most important. According to many color experts we all react in some way to the color around us. Often sick rooms are painted and decorated with this idea in mind, made cheery or quieting or exciting in accordance with the needs of the patients—all with color.

Many of us do not understand color combinations and so do not always choose color correctly. Many books have been written on the subject of color and we could spend a good deal of time studying it. However, for you, books and courses on color would help, but are not necessary to the making of a lovely rug, although a teacher would find all good instructive material helpful. A few simple instructions may help you develop a good color scheme for the contemplated rug. Just by working with colored pieces of cloth and hooking them into flowers, leaves, and scrolls, you gradually become aware of color and develop a taste for good color combinations.

Take a tip from Nature and observe that the larger areas are in subdued tones—the greens, browns, grays, rusts, blues, and golds—while the smaller amounts of bright colors adorn the flowers and birds. The green of the trees and grass covers the hills and valleys. Soil is brown like tree trunks and branches. Rocks are gray, the ocean and sky are blue, while fields of wheat and corn are first green, then golden. These facts are good to remember when planning backgrounds and decorations created against them.

Remember that color comes from the light of the sun. If we never have made an effort to understand color and to apply its lessons to our homes and the clothes we wear, then this is our great chance to begin. Part of the artistry of hooked rugs is an expanding understanding of shade, hue, and tint. Below are some notes on color that may serve as an aid to inspiration.

RED: We know it is used to express danger, fire, aggression, etc. It is not a restful color but has a stimulative effect on some people, irritating on others. Because it is a warm, rich, aggressive color it should be used sparingly.

ORANGE: This is not a restful color and should be used in small quantities. Orange combines the qualities of red or fire—with the sunshine of yellow.

YELLOW: Expresses light, sunshine, and cheerfulness; it is warm and stimulating and may be freely used.

GREEN: Combines the qualities of yellow with the qualities of blue, or the cheerfulness and warmth of yellow with the coolness and reserve of blue. It is quiet, soft, and restful, and is one color that combines easily with any color scheme. Large amounts of yellow greens, spring greens, blue greens, and gray greens may be used in and around the flowers of a rug. Green is the opposite of red.

BLUE: This is a cold color but gives a soothing and restful feeling. It expresses calmness and restraint, poise and dignity.

PURPLE: Expresses mystery, dignity, and mourning. Purple combines the fire of red with the coldness of blue.

RED-BLUE-YELLOW: These are the primary colors, from which all other colors are derived.

ORANGE-GREEN-PURPLE: These are the secondary colors. You combine two primary colors to obtain a secondary color.

YELLOW and BLUE produce GREEN.

RED and YELLOW produce ORANGE.

RED and BLUE produce PURPLE.

COMPLEMENTARY COLORS: If you will look at the color wheel, you will see that colors in opposition are complements to each other, red and green, blue and orange, purple and yellow. Each primary color has a secondary color as its complement. When used next to each other they intensify each other; but as these colors approach one another across the color wheel and meet at the center they become gray. For instance, if you wish to gray yellow you use a bit of purple. (Study color wheel.)

INTERMEDIATE COLORS: These are the colors that come between the primary and secondary colors on the color wheel. These are six: red orange, yellow orange, yellow green, blue green, blue purple, red purple. (See color wheel.)

TRIAD: This term is given to the three colors equidistant on the color wheel, i.e., YELLOW-RED-BLUE or PURPLE-ORANGE-GREEN.

ANALOGOUS: This term is given to two or more colors adjacent on the color wheel but includes only one primary color, i.e., with red are red purple, purple and blue violet; with yellow are yellow green, green and blue green. These groups are analogous colors.

SPLIT COMPLEMENTARY: This term is given to one primary color and the two colors adjacent to its complement, i.e., with RED—blue green and yellow green; with YELLOW—red purple and blue purple.

HUE: Refers to the name of a color, i.e., red, blue, or greenish hue of yellow.

VALUE: Is the degree of lightness or darkness of a color.

38

A STUDY IN COLOR

TINT: Is a lightened value of a color.

SHADE: Is a darkened value of a color.

INTENSITY: This refers to the amount of pure color or the degree of grayness. A color has full intensity when not influenced by gray. As red approaches green on the color wheel it loses its intensity. (See color wheel.) A color is "standard" when not mixed with black or white. A color is of standard intensity when not mixed with its complement.

COLOR HARMONY: Certain colors can live together in harmony because they have a common quality. Pastels are harmonious since they are adjacent on the color wheel. One color in its many values and intensities will live in harmony with the others because they agree.

RHYTHM: Rhythm in color means repetition.

Remember that bright colors may clash if brought together. It is safest to gray all bright colors if they are to be used together. Often colors when used in full strength will give a disagreeable effect.

Color! What a fascinating word! Every experience with color widens one's horizon, one's conception of the very heart of beauty. There are said to be over ten thousand colors, of which the average person knows perhaps less than a hundred. Coloring is limitless in range as even a bit of experimentation in water colors or dyeing will show.

Some people are conscious only of the spectrum colors we all learned in school—red, orange, yellow, green, blue, purple—all of which appear to be different, one from the other, each of which is, nevertheless, capable of being fascinatingly blended through a seemingly endless series of shades. The color wheel is an aid to the fusion of colors.

Keyes & Company of Des Moines, Iowa, offers for one dollar, a color wheel called "The Harmony Selector," with which it is possible, simply by manipulating the three parts of the wheel as directed on each part, to locate and identify triads, complementary, and analogous colors. Such a wheel is of great value to the beginner and experienced rug artist, but especially to the person whose knowledge of color goes no farther than the spectrum range. This wheel, one of the best I have seen because it is so easy to understand, will serve as an excellent guide in planning colors for a rug, flower arrangements, home interiors, and gardens.

Most of us will find that the real joy of all this work is discovery. Almost every home that has children has a box of water colors. Why not get them out as a sort of side issue, using just the primary colors and black and white and see what you can do in producing shades and tints?

The first Cathedral Window shown on the color plate facing page 54 was planned in one lesson and is really a very lovely rug, planned to match another rug done in the same colors. The third Cathedral Window I planned first when the pupil said, "Whatever you think will be best." No definite color scheme was indicated by the pupil, and so I planned this rug with what the pupil had for materials and what I thought would make a lovely rug. However, I was aware that it did not satisfy the pupil and finally got her to admit she did not like the colors I had planned for her, although the girls in the class did and her family also liked it. I discovered in talking to her that her favorite color was blue and so straightway I began to change the colors into what would please her. After many attempts with her limited supply of colors we finally came up with the picture you see here of her rug. How pleased she is with it now, and she did enjoy working on it, simply because the colors suited her and pleased her. She has often said, "Oh, I am so glad we kept at it until we got what *I* liked."

Be happy with the colors you choose for your rug. Make your rug express YOU. The color scheme you choose will play a large part in the beauty of your finished rug.

NOTE: Learn to differentiate between shades of one color. Do not try to combine purple reds with yellow reds in the same flower. Notice in Easter Parade facing page 62 I used different colors harmoniously because one color was present in many of the colors used, i.e., red is the common hue in the yellow reds of the rose, the rust of the wild roses, the purples of the tulips, red browns were used in the background.

VII. *Planning the Rug*

Blessed are the toilers who serve mankind by their labor.

But blessed above all are they whose hands bring forth beauty from the common things that we pass by.

—ROBERT WESTON

TO THE experienced hooker a new pattern is a challenge; it must be met at the earliest possible moment, else it nags the rugger beyond endurance. It inspires the artist in her. The ardent hooker will gaze long and wide eyed at a new pattern, visualizing the finished rug done in colors that suit her taste and needs. She will dream in colors, the hooker's way of

41

"planning"; she will match her skill with that of the challenger, the designer. She will paint in the colors the designer may have seen when she created the design, answering the challenge by creating better, if possible, than the designer could have foreseen. Each new pattern is an unrealized dream, to be realized when finished and found good. When a hooker says, "my fingers fairly itch to get at my newest pattern," she means, literally, what she says.

But you who have never planned a rug, a piece of pattern-stamped burlap may seem a mystery to which you have no key. The burlap and design are baffling; you feel that you must, paradoxically, be an artist before you can plan a rug, while you must also plan a rug before you can be an artist. You should take comfort in a simple fact; every beginning rug artist who has accomplished something has gone through this initial period of confusion. The novice tries, and like any other unaccustomed job that promises never to be easy, its details fall into place and one scarcely realizes the exact moment when it became clear. The novice should also be prepared for a common experience of all ruggers; to find the first finished rug somewhat short of your dreams. The best you can do is strive for your ideal with all your might, and when you are satisfied that you have come as close to it as possible, accept the result as worthy. It may not be as beautiful as it was in your mind, where you "idealized" it, or as lovely as your future rugs will be, but it is a beginning; every beginning is hard, every accomplishment a victory. Every first victory makes a second, and third, easier. Mistakes in the first and subsequent rugs are steppingstones to improvement of successive designs. It is a great joy, shared by all hookers I know, to plan, to create a rug in the ideal, then watch it come alive under the fingers, a thing of beauty. Each new attempt increases the pleasure, never lessens it; the true rug artist never becomes bored.

If you are a novice and have picked a rug for a certain spot in a room, much of the decision as to colors has been made for you. The predominant color in the room is likely to be the rug's predominant color. However, you may discover, when you begin planning, that you don't like the room's predominant color and straightway begin to change it! I am all for such a person, for if your planned rug has made you dissatisfied with a room's predominant color, then your artistry is stirring to new birth, not just for that particular room—which you may now proceed to recolor nearer to your heart's desire—but for the very spirit of the hooker herself. If the predominant color in the room is found to be satisfactory—and you may discover that until you became interested in hooking you never noticed the color scheme of the room!—you then decide whether the color domination proceeds from furniture, draperies, wallpaper, a painting or tapestry, a prize set of china, or antique glass proudly displayed in a corner cupboard that may be visible from anywhere in the room. Whatever the source of dominance that you, definitely searching now, if never before, will quickly discover, this color should determine the predominating colors of the rug. Example: In my dining room for which I am planning a rug with predominating color in blue there is a corner cupboard containing a beautiful set of blue antique china. The soup tureen is proudly displayed on an antique chest. A soft rose is used for painted walls. The rug will carry out this color scheme used in the room.

Many teachers, of whom Mrs. Caroline Saunders is an outstanding example, are able to visualize the ten or twelve or more rugs being planned and worked on in each of her various classes at a given period of instruction. It always seemed miraculous to me when I was a novice, that Mrs. Saunders could say to her pupil, "What color do you wish to predominate?" be told, then look briefly at the design on the frame, and lay out a plan sufficiently explained that you could build a dream that you could call your own. As I look back I realize that much of this early planning emanated from the energetic teacher, though the minds and fingers of the pupils did bring the rugs into finished form. If five, or even more, rugs were of the same design, Mrs. Saunders never planned any two of them alike, so that each had a "personality" of its own when finished. With the predominant color fixed in her mind at a word from her pupil, the whole rug seemed to flash into her mind. I felt that it would be impossible for me to do that; but somehow I do it, though less quickly; and if I can do it, I am sure many others can learn to. All of us can develop this gift of visualization, through trial and error, as I did, without the need of books or a course of lessons, though all aids may prove useful. We can teach ourselves provided we know where to look for inspiration.

If the rug is planned with the predominating color in mind, help for many other colors with which to accent the predominant color may be sought elsewhere. The experienced artist keeps a scrapbook for reference and inspiration. In this scrapbook you should keep many pieces of wallpaper that have appealed—many different designs including geometric, leaf, scroll, scenic— each pattern in many different color schemes. Such treasures will be of great help not only in planning the colors, but many scrolls, leaves, and flowers provide inspiration for the rug evolution of veinings, colorings, and shadings. The more you observe, not necessarily copying the ideas, the more you will find your own ideas awakening—and the more your own ideas will cry out to be tried. The same applies to drapery, slip-cover material, and cretonne. What woman does not enjoy a remnant-counter rummage? Often you will find sample pieces of drapery material, a study of which may show just the right colors or shadings for scrolls or leaves you have in mind for your design. Sometimes you may feel that it is a waste of time rummaging like this when you have no intention of buying; but if you are a persistent person you will often find just what you need, a beautiful piece of material you simply must buy, because it contains a beautiful scroll, or a rose of just the right color to be transferred *in toto* to the new rug design. Materials offer a storehouse of ideas to the searcher. It is not necessary to buy; remember, goods are displayed to be looked at.

You may look and take mental notes and there will never be any real objection if you simply take notes.

I visited the home of a new acquaintance. Such a visit, for me, is always a continuation of the endless search for rug ideas and every angle of rugmaking, from size and shape to design and color. I noted some exquisite needlepoint, full of ideas for beautifully shaded flowers. I asked if I might return with my crayons! My new friend did not mind in the least, believing, as most women do, in sharing beauty proudly.

In another home I found a needlepoint piano bench seat; it contained a poppy shaded in lovely reds, yellow wheat, and bachelor buttons in blue. "Finds" are often encountered thus. This particular needlepoint could be transferred into the beautiful Amber Grain pattern of Mrs. Saunders' design.

Books on flower arrangement are also helpful, containing many ideas for combining colors. Colored prints and painted china are additional treasure-trove possibilities, also complementing flower arrangement books. Many of the new plastic materials and plastic place mats offer some wonderful ideas in flowers and fruits, with helpful suggestions as to shadings. I mention plaid materials again, which might be collected in small samples for reference.

Many books are obtainable, if one has the money to spend; books on color, design, interior decorating may be helpful—however, you may only need to go to the library. Personally I do not believe it is necessary to go to great expense, though a teacher may well find that she needs to augment her knowledge and her files with books that the pupil rug-artist does not require. If you are a beginner you need only to keep your eyes open for the little things that surround you, begging you to dream them into rugs.

Suppose a rug has been selected for a bedroom whose predominating color is blue; possibly blue in the wallpaper, the spreads, the lampshades. We may decide, tentatively, that the rug for this room shall have a blue scroll, or that the outside background will be blue. Next we decide whether the inside background is to be light or dark. It is important to decide what the background color will be, though we do not have the exact tint, shade, or hue on hand; decide if, for example, you want cream, gray, tan, brown, maroon, blue, or black. Many lovely rugs—lovely when visualized—are spoiled by poor choice of background: choice based on ideas I have found that many people share—that once the detail of the rug is done, any old coat or blanket or color will do for the background. The background, you will find, is just as important as any other part of the rug, simply because it is part of the rug. Suppose that eggshell is decided upon as the background—eggshell in the center or outside the scroll, with a small border in blue. Now we look at the wallpaper again. If it is a floral pattern, what are the pattern's complementary colors? Perhaps there are pink or rose shades of dogwood or roses? Then let the center rose of the rug be light to deep rose, the center veining in the scroll deep rose to harmonize with the center flower.

Continuity is of first importance in a rug. The eye of the beholder will follow such continuity, indeed that is the principal reason for it, and if there are no clashes, no color conflicts, if, in short, the rug has been carefully and painstakingly planned, then the beholder likes the rug, perhaps without being able to explain why. Mrs. Saunders always taught her pupils—a practice I have since followed, as do most teachers who learned from Caroline Saunders —to plan border or scroll and floral design in the center, with some continuity of shade or hue of one color. The reason is obvious, once you are aware of it: the rug pleases, is in harmony with itself!

The central rose, then the leaves; if the rug has many leaves, or many kinds of leaves, the decision will be, usually, that many greens will be used to bring out the flowers, to set them off, to frame them. Green is the one color that can be used with many other colors, so one should select many greens with confidence that there is very little likelihood of going very far wrong. Yellow greens, blue greens, spring or forest greens, gray greens—all can be used in the leaves in a given rug. You should freely make use of all that appeal to you, not confining yourself to any one green, since Nature herself does not. You will also notice, quite early in your researches, that in many kinds of drapery material the artist who planned the color scheme did not hesistate to invent blue leaves, purple leaves, rose, brown, or leaves of any color she needed in her scheme at the moment. It is the color scheme that is important, not that the resulting leaves be exactly as they are in Nature. There are many leaves of many colors in Nature that the artist will never see! It is even likely that those she invents will be found in Nature some day! If a rug can be made lovelier, more harmonious, with blue leaves, then blue leaves should by all means be hooked. If the hooker cannot copy Nature always, Nature may somewhere copy the rugger after all.

If the plan calls for blue in the rug's scroll, then let there be some blue in the center, in some of the flowers; a bit of yellow and orchid, or the red purple or plum shades, would help to make a beautiful center. A light background, or if you prefer a deeper tone, may be used under the flowers. This makes a more striking rug, bringing out the colors more vividly. I find it helpful, while dreaming out a color scheme, to place swatches of color around on the stamped burlap pattern, moving them to suit my dreams, inspired by the swatches that seem to tell me what to dream next, to try this or that combination. When I have exhausted all the possibilities of actually shifting colors, have set upon some colors as being just what I want, I color in some of the design with hard pastel crayons—excellent aids to visualization. This kind of experimentation also helps in color balancing.

Additional hints: if a yellow flower is used at one end of a floral design, then that color, if not the same flower, may be used somewhere on the opposite end of the rug, to balance. The triangle arrangement is good, too, i.e., if a yellow flower is used at the center of one end of the rug, two yellow flowers may corner the rug at the other end—a triangle suggested by the three points of the triad of flowers.

You might wish to make one of the Currier & Ives scenes like "Home for Thanksgiving" or "Mr. and Mrs. Currier." Colored pictures may often be found on Christmas cards, calendars, and I have even found them on place mats. I always keep any Christmas cards that have helpful ideas on winter snow scenes with buildings, animals, sleighs, etc. I also like to collect colored pictures and Christmas cards that may have good ideas on trees, the sky, mountains—anything that will give me ideas on perspective. You will find many helpful ideas for doing nursery scenes in children's books, for example the "Little Boy Blue" rug.

VIII. *Hooking Technique*

All our progress is an unfolding; like a vegetable bud you
have first an instinct, then an opinion, then a knowledge.

—Ralph Waldo Emerson

NOTE: *Tear all material to be used in hooking on the straight of goods before
cutting by machine or by hand,* so finely cut strips will not pull apart. If
your material is the least bit off the straight of the goods or on the bias
your strips will pull apart.

1. Hold hook in palm of hand (sketch #1). You will find as you become
accustomed to this position that it enables you to work with a wrist movement that is generally faster, less tiring, and provides more technical control; loops can be drawn through more easily. If you use your fingers to
hold the hook as you do in crocheting, your fingers grow tired and you
cannot work as fast. Persistent development of the wrist movement technique will, I believe, prove to be preferable.

47

2. Your other hand holds and guides the strip of material. Thumb and fore-finger hold the material, which may additionally be held between the third and fourth fingers. I find this helps to control the height of the loops drawn through the burlap and keeps them uniform, though thumb and forefinger are enough (sketch #1). It also helps to keep material from twisting.

3. The hand holding the material is placed underneath, up against the under-side of the burlap, under that part of the design you wish to hook (sketch #3). Be careful not to allow material to bunch underneath; keep it smooth against the burlap.

4. The hook, with point away from you, goes down through the burlap mesh, picks up the end of the material (which to start with is held over finger—sketch #2), pulling through to the top for about one-fourth to one-half inch (this end will be clipped even with the loops) then the hook goes through next mesh in burlap and pulls up a loop *one-eighth inch high*. Continue to hook the rest of the strip of material, pulling the other end through the burlap (sketch #4). *Remember, all ends are pulled through to right side of burlap; there should be no ends left on the wrong side of the rug.* The two ends are clipped off even with the loops. *Do not clip loops.*

5. Hook according to the weight of the material. If thin material is used then you will have to go in almost every mesh of the burlap *(if you are cutting your strips one-eighth of an inch)*. When you use heavier or wider material you will have to skip a few spaces. *Never pack* or your rug will be stiff. (The life of a rug depends upon the life of the backing—if you overload your backing your rug will not wear as well.) But if, on the other hand, you skip too many places as I have seen some of my pupils do, simply because I warned them not to pack their loops, then you may have the sorrowing experience that your rug will not wear as well either. If you skip too much then the loops may pull out. You need to experiment on your own and decide what is best. *Remember,* however, that as long as *one loop touches the next one* you are hooking about right.

6. By holding material between thumb and forefinger (and if you prefer, tightly with the third and fourth fingers) you move the hand along under the burlap, while the hand holding the hook works with a twisting, pull-ing movement as it picks up the material and draws it through to the top of the pattern. The twist of the wrist as you work releases the loop from the hook, enabling you to pick up the next loop quickly (sketch #4).

7. While hooking in one direction, never cross over underneath as you do in

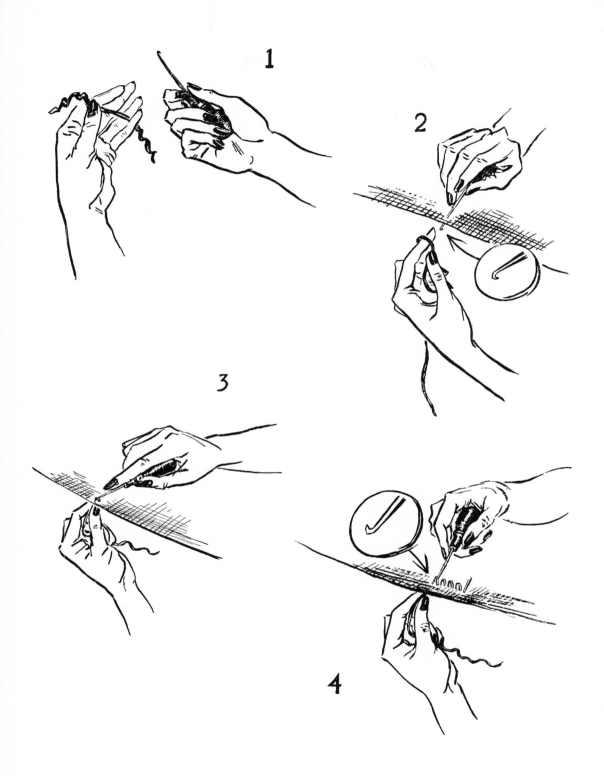

some kinds of needlework. Always clip your material where you wish to end and then start in another direction.

8. Never hook in straight lines unless you are doing the outside border, borders in Oriental or geometric designs, etc. When you hook all of your rug in straight lines as I have seen many women do—hooking straight and even right across the burlap—this gives a very set look to your rug and does not give the artistic and professional look for which you should strive. Leaves and flowers are hooked according to the contour of the petals or veinings. The background is hooked by following the contour of the outer edge of flowers, leaves and scroll, perhaps for a few times, then changing and going in another direction. *Do not hook backgrounds in straight lines.*

9. If you are a beginner and have never tried to hook before, then it is a good idea to start anywhere on the background of design and practice hooking until you have acquired the very simple technique of hooking. At first you may find it easier to try hooking in a straight line just for practice. Once you have mastered the technique of hooking and pulling your loops through evenly and just the right height, start hooking in wavy or curved lines, or follow the outline of a scroll or leaf. The above rule applies to material for background. If, however, you are going to use two different shades of material with the intention of forming blocks or circles or diamonds, or making a mosaic design, then, of course, you hook your lines accordingly. It is not always possible to get just the right color or weave of material you would like for a background. I think backgrounds are very important and I have seen more than one rug spoiled by poor choice of background color and texture of material. If you love hooking as much as most of us do, then you will constantly be on the lookout for good background colors and weaves. Some women wait until they start a rug or until it is nearly finished before they become concerned with background material, and with so many women hooking these days it is not always easy to find. So it is a good plan to buy, borrow, or beg if you have to, background material for not only the rug you plan to make but for many future rugs. Lovely old homespun blankets that have seen their best days may still be good enough for that rug. I don't mean to cut up perfectly good blankets, but when I see some people using the old homespun blanket for padding ironing boards, I feel I am not committing a great sin to cut one up and hook it in a rug.

Always strive for perfection. Work with finely cut strips of material, hook through almost every mesh of the burlap and with a low pile. Remember to bring all ends up to the right side of the rug. Do not pack and do not clip loops.

Hook in the manner prescribed above and your rug will last for many, many years, giving you good service continually. The reason that these rugs will last is because they are made of either new or good woolen materials on good quality burlap, cut in fine strips, and drawn not too high through almost every mesh of the burlap and not clipped, thus achieving a firm tight nap that will stand wear, vacuuming, and other cleaning methods without loops pulling out. If the strips are too wide, hooking, of necessity, must be high and too many spaces skipped; or if packed in every mesh, it will add weight to the backing causing it to wear out faster than a low-pile rug. Also there is no opportunity for detail work as compared to hooking with fine strips. Many such rugs when shaken or vacuumed, will cause the loops gradually to work free and if the burlap is of poor quality and starts to fray, it becomes almost impossible to mend. Thus, attention to all details pays off in the beauty of the final result. Perfection of detail and painstaking workmanship produce lovely, praiseworthy rugs, any one of which may become an heirloom for your descendants or a museum piece, long after you are gone.

Mrs. Saunders always cites the original Lucy Baker rug, which is over 120 years old and still in perfect condition. It was hooked with a very low pile.

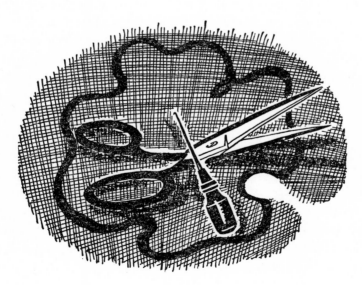

IX. Cathedral Window

Nothing makes the soul so pure, so religious,
as the endeavor to create something perfect.

—MICHELANGELO

I DO not believe there is a more beautiful geometric repeat rug pattern than the Cathedral Window. It was chosen for this book not only because of its lovely design but because it gives the beginner a chance to hook a beautiful rug without having to plan too many colors or to learn to do the more difficult job of shading. It is proved again that we of today have more opportunities for self-expression than our rugmaking forebears because science has given us more conveniences—especially in the field of color. We covered the matter of color in a previous chapter, but it would not be amiss to give some information here that will serve to increase interest in visualizing and appreciating the Cathedral Window.

Dyes, color mixtures, and blends were something for pioneers to find for themselves by personal systems of trial and error. Dyes and colors from England required weeks en route and housewives could not wait. They experimented with plants and flowers and borrowed what they could from Indian lore. Many New England housewives raised indigo plants for dye in their gardens. All we have to do is select and experiment and that only if we crave the fun and excitement of the joy our forebears experienced when something they tried produced beautiful results.

Now we can buy dyes and colored swatches to aid us in attaining beautiful results. For the purpose of this chapter on the Cathedral Window, let us assume that every reader who is interested has, or can obtain, the necessary colors. If you haven't, you can substitute and come up with *a* Cathedral Window very likely more beautiful than the ones shown here.

The plate facing page 54 shows three differently planned color schemes for the Cathedral Window, none of which have to be followed. They are given only as steppingstones, as guideposts to your own Cathedral Windows. If instructions herein seem confusing, read slowly, take it a step at a time, and let the Cathedral Window burst forth upon your mind like an opening bud, for that's how rug artistry is developed. You will be able if you take these instructions slowly, carefully, to make a lovely Cathedral Window rug. Having made one you will, I am sure, be tempted to start some other pattern at once.

The Cathedral Window offers you an excellent chance to perfect your hooking technique without concentrating on the more difficult job of shading. You must learn to hook inside the lines, so as not to overcrowd or pack too much material into each section. Remember that instructions herein given call for material to be cut about one eighth of an inch in width. Thus most sections will take only two rows of hooking, with extra loops added at corners or in the wider sections.

Paisley is excellent for this particular pattern, but hunting for the right material persistently may produce something you will prefer, perhaps a plaid that suits your color scheme better than any Paisley. Paisley is just a starting suggestion. I'd advise using a plaid that has many colored threads woven into small blocks. Large blocks of plaid do not produce the effect of a stained-glass window; Paisley does.

I feel that a light-colored plain material is better for the background. A mixed background detracts from the cumulative effect of the design itself.

The colored pictures and directions herein, accord with Mrs. Caroline Saunders' preferred theory of uniformity in this particular pattern—with which I agree. I mention this because there is a divergence of opinion among teachers, which is certain to come to the attention sooner or later of the researching rug artist, who hold that each separate motif of the Cathedral Window should be done in a different color scheme. To my mind that seems entirely too "busy," though I do not decry the idea if you prefer it that way, simply because my own choice is different. Again we accent personal desire in rugs to be achieved. Each of us expresses herself in her own way and is repeatedly urged in this book to do so. I feel, however, that no part of such rug, emphasizing the fact that this is purely personal with me, has a finished appearance. The whole effect is to hit the beholder in the face, almost as a physical shock. It doesn't soothe, it expresses discord rather than harmony, and this seems to be true no matter what colors are chosen. If several color schemes are used in each motif the rug has the appearance of a number of unfinished Cathedral Windows that have somehow melted and run together.

Now let's plan the three Cathedral Windows pictured with this chapter. First, note the sketch of a section of a Cathedral Window, the areas between the lines carefully numbered, as are the ovals, squares, and rectangles. These numbers are analogous to those in each set of directions for each Cathedral Window. The color scheme of each Cathedral Window is illustrated in the three-colored chart of materials used, facing page 56.

CATHEDRAL WINDOW NO. I

Colored Chart #1

Paisley colors: wine, rose, a green turquoise, and white.

The color scheme of this rug was planned on the colors found in the Paisley shawl.

1. Outline in black.
2. Fill in with Paisley or plaid. Study the sketch and notice that this #2 follows completely around the motif. This same #2 material is used to fill in the center arcs of the motif that are outlined in black. On the burlap pattern the circles are completely drawn through these arcs. However, these lines are not to be hooked into the arcs. The arcs are filled in solidly with #2 and the lines are not hooked in.

CATHEDRAL WINDOW, *hooked by Mrs. Emma Storb,*
Mrs. Vera Underhill and Mrs. Musser Stauffer

Corner Motif of "Cathedral Window" Rug

3. Fill in with turquoise.
4. Fill in with a maroon and white herringbone tweed.
5. Fill in with a wine and green turquoise plaid, outlined in black.
(Notice on colored photograph of this rug we used plaid only in four outer corner blocks. The other #5 blocks were hooked in three shades of rose from dark to light in center.)
6. Fill in with a rose shade, outline in black.
7. Hook one row of dark green turquoise (or Rockwell's Aqua swatch #11).
Hook one row of medium green turquoise (or Rockwell's Aqua swatch #11).
Hook two rows of a lighter green turquoise (or Rockwell's Aqua swatch #11).
8. Hook one row of deep burgundy.
Hook two rows of wine.
9. Hook two rows of deep rose (or Rockwell's swatch #3).
10. Hook two rows of medium rose (or Rockwell's swatch #3).
11. Hook about four rows of light aqua, or two different shades of light aqua or turquoise.
BACKGROUND: Cream.
BORDER: Wine.

NOTE: Remember the above directions are numbered to correspond to the parts of the sketch with the same number; they also correspond to the same numbers on the colored plates of materials used. Thus #1 on the color plate shows you a black material, and in the above directions #1 tells you to outline in black and on the sketch you will find where you are to use the black material to outline by #1 with an arrow pointing to outline.

CATHEDRAL WINDOW NO. 2

1. Outline in black.
2. Fill in with Paisley or plaid.
3. Fill in with teal, about two rows. (Around corners three rows.)
4. Fill in with a gold tweed, two rows, possibly three rows.
5. Fill in with a teal, rust, and brown tweed, outlined in black.
6. Fill in with a bright gold or mustard color, outlined in black.
7. Fill in with teal and black herringbone tweed or plaid (three or four rows). (I used one darker shade and one a little lighter.)
8. Fill in with turquoise or two shades of turquoise (two or three rows).

"Cathedral Window"

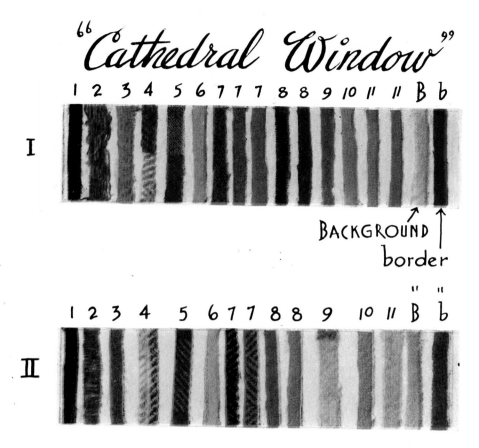

1 2 3 4 5 6 7 7 8 8 9 10 11 11 B b

I

BACKGROUND
border

1 2 3 4 5 6 7 7 8 8 9 10 11 " B " b

II

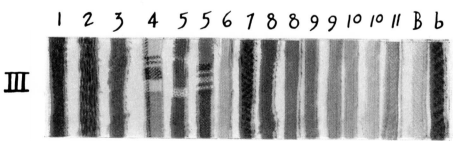

1 2 3 4 5 5 6 7 8 8 9 9 10 10 11 " B " b

III

COLOR CHART FOR CATHEDRAL WINDOW

PHOTO BY H. LANDIS

CATHEDRAL WINDOW

9. Fill in with yellow and brown plaid or herringbone (two or three rows).
10. Fill in with light blue or a lighter shade of turquoise (two or three rows).
11. Fill in with a pinkish tan shade (four or five rows).
    BORDER: Teal or dark green turquoise.
    BACKGROUND: Light gray.

CATHEDRAL WINDOW NO. 3

Paisley colors: red, blue, white, deep gold.

1. Outline in navy.
2. Fill in with Paisley.
3. Fill in with old blue.
4. Fill in with a plaid. The one used here was red and white with a green and black stripe (with a lot of white).
5. Fill in with a plaid outlined in black (there are two pieces shown on colored chart of materials used because one piece did not show all the colors in the plaid). The colors of plaid were bright blue, red, and greenish blue. Notice #5 in center on colored photograph of rugs and you will see that we did not use the plaid in center marked #5 but used instead the same colors as #10 below.
6. Fill with gold, outlined in black.
7. Fill in with dark blue and black tweed, about two rows.
8. Fill in with old blue, two rows.
9. Fill in with two rows of a lighter blue.
10. Fill in with from three to four rows of Rockwell's bronze swatch #8, hooking from the dark to light shade. This color is a shade resembling a peach tint or very light rusty peach, or cinnamon.
11. Hook about four rows of a light blue, or same as #9.
    BACKGROUND: Light cream.
    BORDER: Old blue tweed.

X. *Easter Parade*

O thou sculptor, painter, poet,
Take this lesson to thy heart;
That is best which liest nearest;
Shape from that thy work of art.

—LONGFELLOW

AMONG the many beautiful Heirloom floral designs, I have selected the Easter Parade for this book. The beauty of its design is a lure to the hooker whether she is a novice or an experienced artist. It is a kind of bait, like every lovely design. This kind of bait is inspiration. Usually the hooker cannot rest until she has manifested it in color. To the rug-artist all new patterns are intriguing and there is a yearning to capture rich colors, bringing them out of her dreams to work into such lovely designs.

Usually on my visits home I love to call on some of my old friends who are ardent rug-hookers, just so we can talk rugs. One evening while I was passing the home of a particular friend, I noticed the lights on and decided to stop for a few minutes. I rang the bell, and receiving no answer decided to try the back door, but as I was passing the sun porch I saw friend hubby hooking on his wife's latest rug, Easter Parade, totally oblivious to the phone or doorbell! Believe it or not but our very masculine friend has finished several of his own rugs and they are indeed rugs to be proud of! Not all husbands get hooked into the hooking business but almost all of them take a keen interest in the rug their wives are hooking. In fact one husband of note is more critical than his wife, and so I find I must plan rugs to please the husbands, too!

The color scheme used in the Easter Parade opposite page 60 was planned to fit a corner of my living room. An old needlepoint tapestry wall hanging as well as the colors used in my living room provided the inspiration for this lovely rug. The room's colors centered around the tans and browns of the different wood, the lovely 20 x 30-foot hand-pegged oak flooring, the reddish-brown deep window sills, the corner cupboards in their natural wood finish, the light and dark mahogany furniture, the gold-colored curtains, and the green walls. For complementary colors and accents I used many shades of rust, red, gold, yellow, green, salmon, and red purple in the flowers and leaves. These same colors were also found in the needlepoint tapestry. A scroll border shaded from gold to dark rust, and in the picture many shades of tan, brown, mahogany, rust, salmon, red, and red purple were used for accents. I repeatedly find that needlepoint pieces both new and old offer a wealth of ideas, in color schemes and in shading. Recently a kind friend showed me her collection of old German needlepoint patterns, all beautifully shaded in colors. What a treasure!

The directions for making the rug are given to you in detail and if the colors I have chosen do not please you or suit your needs then maybe the colors used in one of the other pictures will be an inspiration—will help you to decide your own color scheme. Not only is there a colored photograph of this rug given you but a color plate of all the materials used in making this pattern. I felt that in showing you the actual colored pieces of material used, you would find them to be of more value than to say, "Use an Aqualon Blue or Terra Cotta shade." Would you know what shade I meant? I have so often asked pupils of mine in class to bring me their yellow greens, and not knowing color perhaps they bring a blue green. A colored picture is helpful in planning your own color schemes but you cannot tell all the different shades that are used to make each flower, for often they are so close that they fuse into each other and are lost to the eye.

The color plate of materials used is marked with numbers for your convenience in following the corresponding numbers on the sketches. I believe that you will find the sketches to be of great help in the making of your Easter Parade and possible future rug patterns. They should aid you in understanding the shading of your flowers, leaves, etc. First, on every sketch there is a pattern of the flower exactly as it appears on the burlap pattern, with the petals marked A, B, C, etc., to aid you in following the written instructions given on the opposite page. This is referred to as sketch #1. Now sketch #2 is the key to shading, showing you how to work the colors shown on the color plate for each particular flower, with corresponding numbers, for #1 on the color chart of materials refers also to #1 on the key, of sketch #2. This same key also shows you how to hook from light to dark and the direction in which to hook your lines. Sketch #3 is given to show you how the finished flower will look. This sketch gives you the effect of light and dark but will not show clearly all the different shades used. The key is for six shades, as most flowers need between five and six shades to produce the effect you wish. However, for some flowers, such as the large rose, I used nine shades of red but have marked some of these shades as alternates, so you can use, for example, I or Ia, or both, as you prefer. On a few flowers I have used only five shades. I mention this so you will understand why, on the color chart of materials, some of the numbers read 1, 2, 4, 5, 6, omitting 3 or some other number.

You will find the word "dovetail" given in the directions, and to clarify this term in case you are confused by it, you dovetail one shade of color in between another shade, i.e., if you form a V-shape of #5, then bring #4 down into the V, #4 will not come down as far as #5 but it will extend in the other direction a little farther.

Learn to squint at your flowers while trying to shade. You will see perspective better. Also after hooking for a while, tilt frame upright, and stand off away from rug to observe it from a distance. You will find that perspective becomes clearer to you at a distance.

SCROLLS

Scrolls should be the keynote of the color scheme of our rug. Usually a scroll will carry the predominating color around which the rug is built. It is the frame for the floral center but it should never be so bright or harsh that

EASTER PARADE, *hooked by Vera Underhill*

it will take your attention away from the lovely flowers in the center. Your flowers should carry the secondary and complementary colors, also the accents. The veins and outlines of the scroll also pick up the accents and the complementary colors. Once again I call your attention to the plaids that are so wonderful for planning many rugs and can be used in working out the scroll, for often in using a plaid you will have the color scheme of your rug all planned for you. You may pick a color in the plaid to vein and to outline the scroll. Remember that veining in both scroll and leaves should be as a rule a bright contrasting color. Otherwise, when the other colors are worked in around it, it may become lost.

There are many ways to work out the colors for a scroll. I do not attempt to give the impression that any of my ideas are better, but I remind you again that this book is being written for the novice who tries to hook rugs without the aid of a teacher; I only suggest what can be done, hoping that the ideas given here may be the springboards to the beginner's own creative expression. Attending rug exhibits and working in groups with other hookers if you have no teacher help to increase your own storehouse of ideas, which may be used in preference to mine.

Many pupils who come to me for lessons have no plaids or tweeds to work out the scrolls in their rug patterns. I find such materials to be the easiest for beginners to work with, for you only need three different materials, one color for the veining, one for the outline, and the plaid or tweed to fill in the remainder of the scroll. If you try to use three shades of a plain color in a large scroll you will find it difficult to make it look well. It will have a jumpy effect instead of a gradual blending of many shades of a plain color, from light to dark. A pupil of mine is using Cushing's mahogany dye to dye her material for this scroll in Easter Parade. She is using ten shades, from the lightest tint down to the deepest shade, and veining it with a chartreuse. It makes a very lovely scroll.

If you have very few colors with which to work, I would suggest you dye materials to use Plan No. 1, which is what I used in my Easter Parade. But if you have a tweed or plaid, then work out Plan No. 2, using only a contrast for veining and another color for outlining the scroll. Study Mrs. Smith's Plume Leaf Runner following page 14 for additional ideas on how to hook with tweeds. Of course this is a black and white photograph and will not give you color combinations but may help in showing you how to treat leafy scrolls, with tweed materials.

NOTE: For beginners I think it is easier to start hooking the scroll because once your scroll is planned you can go ahead and hook without concentrating too much on the problems of shading such as the flowers require.

Hook scroll first, then flowers, and leaves, then work in your background. A clever hooker will use a darker background under the flowers, as it gives depth. If you are clever you can improve the design by making the spaces between flowers and leaves inconspicuous.

SCROLL PLAN No. 1

NOTE: If you study the sketch before working out this plan it will help you to understand the directions. In order not to confuse you we have kept the key throughout all the sketches, from #1 to #6 referring to from one to six shades. The scroll in Plan No. 1 on the color chart of materials used, on the facing page, shows you eleven shades, but for your convenience we (referring to the artist and me) have marked on the left side of the veining (which is marked #6) five light shades for the scroll, numbered accordingly from #1 to #5. Then on the right side of the veining are five dark shades, ranging from the lightest dark shade to the deepest shade and also numbered from #1 to #5. Now study the sketch and notice that we have marked Plan No. 1 on the right-hand side of the sketch and that on either side of the veining is marked small (a) and (b). Where small (a) is found on the sketch you will hook on this side the lightest shades of your scroll colors, the lightest #1 shade on the outer edge of the scroll and working in to the #5 shade next to the veining. Then on the other side of the veining, where you find the small (b) you will hook the darkest shades of the scroll colors, but working the #1 shade next to the veining and bringing the darkest shade #5 at the outer edge of the scroll. On this side of Scroll Plan No. 1 we have colored black to show you this is the outer edge of the rug pattern and is hooked in a darker color if you prefer.

1. Hook #6 for center veining and side veinings.
2. Hook #1 of the lighter shades from point A around to point B. You may continue around to point D (although this is not shown on sketch).
3. Hook #2 next to #1 from point A around to B as shown in sketch.
4. Hook #3 from point A around to B following #2.
5. Hook #4 from point A around to B following #3.
6. Hook #5 from point A around to B following #4 and next to the veining.

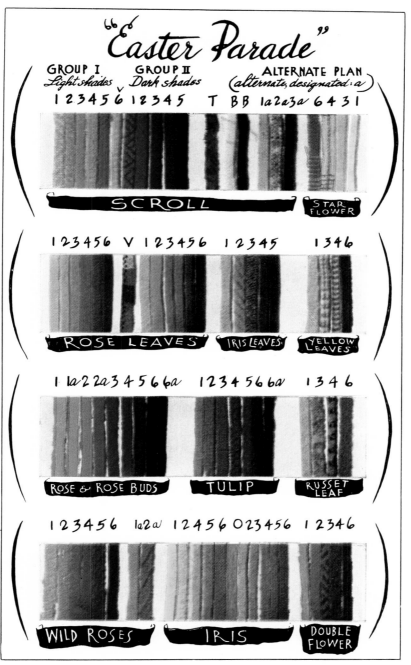

COLOR CHART FOR EASTER PARADE

PHOTO BY H. LANDIS

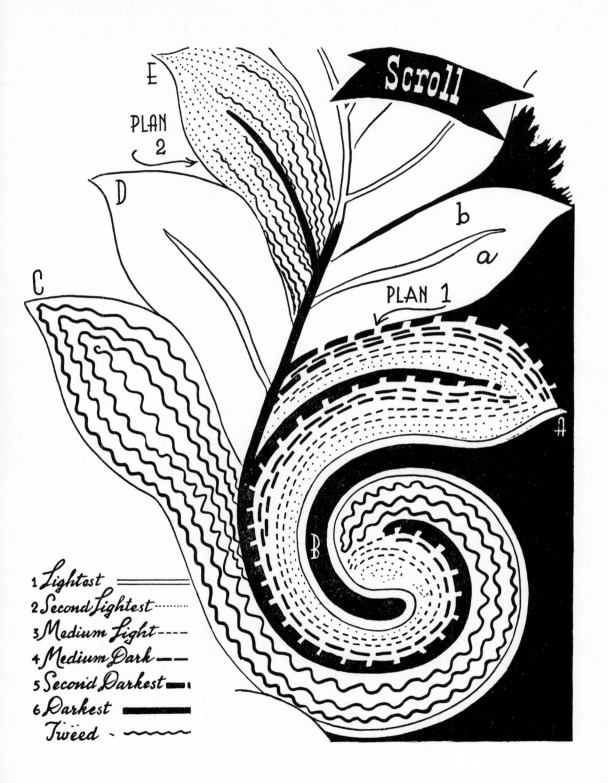

Scroll

E

PLAN 2

D

C

PLAN 1

b

a

A

B

1 Lightest ————
2 Second Lightest ·········
3 Medium Light - - - -
4 Medium Dark — —
5 Second Darkest ▬▬
6 Darkest ━━━━
Tweed ∿∿∿

The above directions follow on each of the leafy sections of this scroll, only the lines are brought just to the center veining as you can see, unless you wish to achieve the effect of a darker base as I did on my pattern from C to B. This tends to give weight to the base of scroll and to achieve balance. It is best to use a darker tweed, and you hook from point B between veining and outer edge to point C and follow the wavy lines shown in the sketch. You may add the side veining in C if you wish. I did not add it in mine, for after trying it I decided it looked better without the side veining. (This is a preference only; you may hook all sections of scroll as in A.)

7. Now start hooking on small (b) with the darker shades and start with #1, the lightest of the dark shades, hooking this #1 shade right next to the center veining.
8. Hook #2 next to #1.
9. Hook #3 next to #2 (bringing each line out a little farther toward point of scroll).
10. Hook #4 next to #3.
11. Hook #5, the darkest shade, along edge of scroll as shown in sketch. Continue the above plan in all sections of scroll.

SCROLL PLAN No. 2

1. Vein scroll in contrasting color such as green or bright rust or gold (both center veining and side veining). 3a on color chart.
2. Work a brown and yellow or rust tweed at the base of sections from center veining, fanning the lines out a little, and varying the length as shown by wavy lines in sketch (2a on color chart, facing page 62).
3. Use a lighter shade or lighter contrast such as gold for the tips, working it down between the tweed as shown (1a on color chart). See Plume Leaf Runner, after page 14, for ideas on working out tweeds in a leafy scroll.

OPEN WILD ROSE

1. Edge each petal with #1, the lightest shade, as shown in sketch, remembering that where one petal overlaps another the edging shade, or #1, is hooked completely around the petal on top, such as petal E, overlaps petals A and D; use edging shade on petals A and D, only from point where it meets E.
2. The tips of petals A and C curl over, so fill in this part with #1 the lightest shade as shown in sketch.

64

Wild Rose

Hook according to the lines shown here ↓

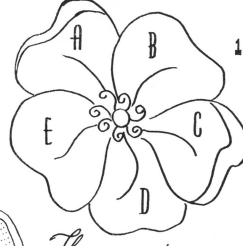

Flower as it appears on rug pattern

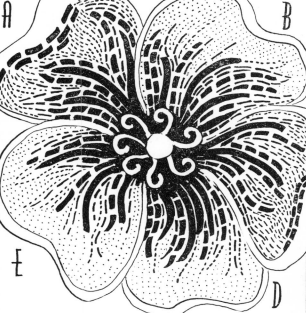

Finished flower

1. Lightest ═══════
2. Second Lightest ···········
3. Medium Light - - - - - - -
4. Medium Dark — — — —
5. Second Darkest ▬ ▬ ▬ ▬
6. Darkest ▬▬▬▬▬▬

3. It is best to hook stamens before these delicate lines are lost under adjacent hooking; you could use a soft green.

4. Fill center with a soft yellow or yellow and brown plaid, a flecked, or checked material.

5. For the center veinings hook #6, the darkest shade, remembering to curve your lines slightly.

6. On either side of this center veining I add (although this is not drawn in on pattern) another shorter veining in #6, the darkest shade. These lines should come together at the base of petal and fan out, curving the lines with the contour of the petal or veining (center veining).

7. On petal A observe that one side of E and B petals lies on top of A; so hook both #5 and #6 from base of A, keeping these darker shades right next to the edging shade on E and B. Be sure to hook your lines with a slight curve and vary the length, never end all lines of the same shade at the same length from center out toward edge of petal. Keep petals A and C—with tip-over—darker than the other petals.

8. Now petal C lies on top of petals B and D and is edged with #1 all around to center. On petals B and D hook #6 or #5 shade near this edging. This is to give the effect of the petal on top casting a shadow on the one underneath.

9. On petals B, E, and D, hook #5 shade, dovetailing this shade between #6 shade. Start #5 where the veinings #6 come together and extend further than the veinings.

10. Now hook #4 shade, dovetailing it between #5 shade, extending lines as shown.

11. Now hook #3 shade, dovetailing it between the #4 shade.

12. In the spaces left and along the edging hook #2 shade, dovetailing it in between #3 shade, bringing the lines down at different lengths as shown.

13. On petals A and C, hook #5 or #4 shade for depth, right along under the curled part of the petal. This is another instance of a dark shade producing a shadow, making the light portion appear to be on top.

14. Fill the bases of these two petals with more of #5 and #4 shades and dovetail the remaining spaces with #3, omit #2 on these petals only.

NOTE: There are two alternate shades, #1a and #2a, that I used in center flowers.

Double Flower

1

2

3

1 *Lightest*
2 *Second Lightest*
3 *Medium Light*
4 *Medium Dark*
5 *Second Darkest*
6 *Darkest*

DOUBLE FLOWER

NOTE: This flower is called a double flower for as you can see, four center petals lie atop six lower petals. (Only five shades were used; you may use six if you prefer.)

1. Edge all petals with #1 as shown in sketch.
2. In petals D and H there are tip-overs; fill in these tip-overs with #1 as shown in sketch.
3. Directly under the tip-over in petals D and H hook #5 shade or #6 for shadow line.
4. In petal B you will notice almost the whole petal is turned over. This is filled with #1 (I used a piece of material dyed to give mottled effect rather than plain material).

Petals A-C-D:
5. Hook center veinings of #6, adding more than one as I have done.
6. Hook #5 or #4 between #6 starting at base and fanning out as shown.
7. Dovetail #3 between #5 and #4.
8. On petals A and C hook #2 in remaining spaces. Omit #2 on petal D with tipover.

Petals E-F-G-H-J-K:
1. Hook #6 or #5 at base of each petal and a little along the edging of inside petals. Curve your lines with contour of petal. Bring #6 up into petals for veinings.
2. Hook #4 between #5 and #6.
3. Hook #3 next to #4.
4. On petal H hook all remaining space with #3.
5. On all other petals hook #2 in remaining spaces.

STAR FLOWER

1. Vein each petal with #1 shade. Do not make this a straight line but curve it slightly with contour of outer edge of petal.
2. Edge each petal with #6 as shown in #2 sketch.
3. When one petal overlaps another as petal A overlaps petal B and F, then edge petal A to center and petals B and F only to where they meet petal A.
4. Next to #6 on petal A hook #4, following contour of #6.

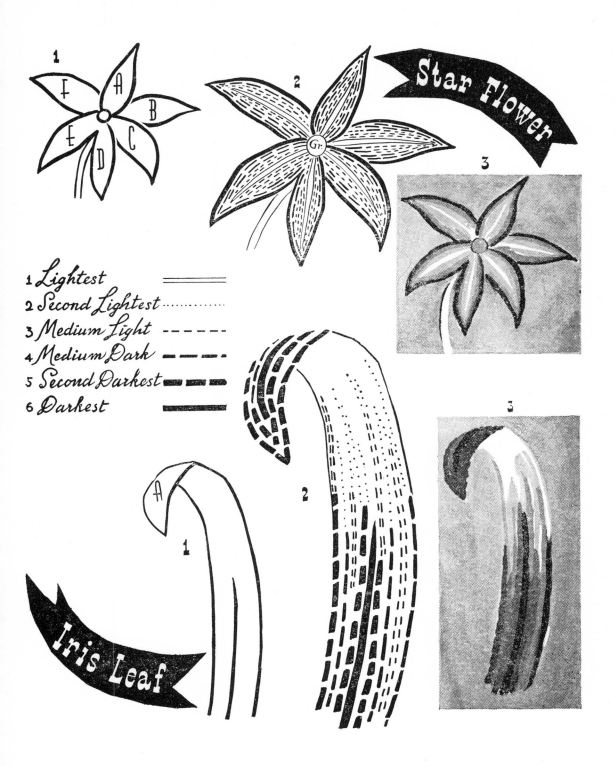

1

F A
B
E C
D

2

Gr.

3

1 *Lightest* —————
2 *Second Lightest* ·············
3 *Medium Light* — — — —
4 *Medium Dark* — — —
5 *Second Darkest* ━ ━ ━
6 *Darkest* ━━━━

A

1

2

3

Iris Leaf

5. Next to #4 on petal A hook #3.
6. Hook in center some yellow green or soft green plaid or checked material.
7. Follow above procedure for each petal.
   Only four shades were used in this small flower.

NOTE: Assuming that you are using a light background, it is best when using a light shade, such as yellow, to work a darker shade on the edge and vein it with a lighter shade, as I have done here. If your background is dark then you may reverse the plan, having #1 for edge and #5 or #6 for veinings. You may also hook the petal on top in all lighter shades and hook the one underneath in all darker shades, especially phlox and verbena or other groupings of flowers.

IRIS LEAVES

1. Vein these leaves with a dark olive green #6 or a contrasting color such as rust or plaid material as I have done—this veining is not shown in color chart with iris leaf colors, but with rose leaves.
2. For the tip-over, hook the veining in first if it is shown in pattern, then hook rest of the tip-over in #5 or #6 shades as shown in sketch.
3. Hook #1 the lightest shades (as shown in sketch) next to tip-over.
4. Hook #5 at the base of leaf next to veining and at outer edges varying the length of lines as shown.
5. Hook #4 next to #5, following the contour of veining.
6. Hook #2 between lines of #1.
7. Hook #3 between #4 and #2.

NOTE: Do not make all the leaves the same; a more interesting effect will result if you vary the way you hook your leaves. Make some with dark tip-overs and some with light tip-overs. When you reverse the above procedure and make a light tip-over, then keep your leaf dark.

In hooking stems of flowers and leaves, be careful not to hook them in light shades since they become lost. They may be brown or rust or green. I do not like to hook two rows for stems, rather I cut material a little wider than usual and hook only one row.

RUST IRIS

NOTE: There are many ways to hook an iris. I would suggest that you get your scrapbook of ideas out and look at all the pictures and paintings of irises, then

70

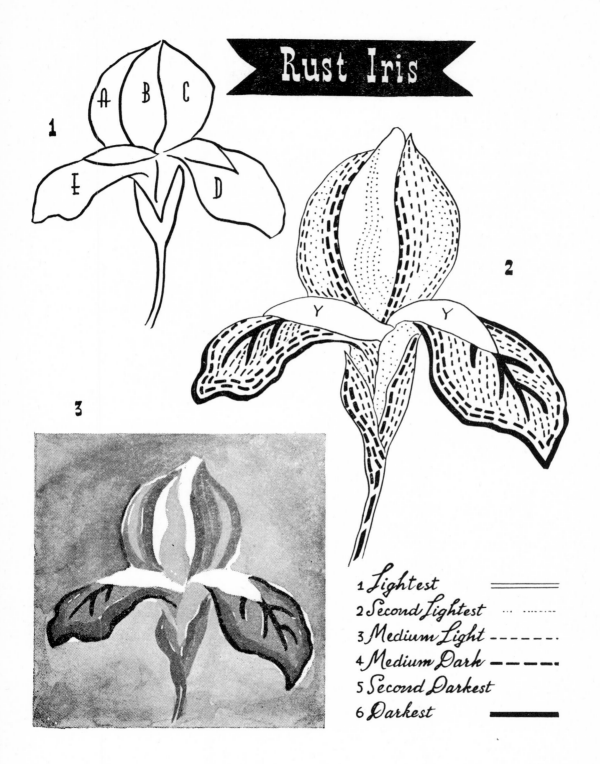

Rust Iris

1

A B C
E D

2

Y Y

3

1 Lightest
2 Second Lightest
3 Medium Light
4 Medium Dark
5 Second Darkest
6 Darkest

choose the color scheme best suited to your needs. Some iris are made with light standards and dark falls or both standards and falls made in same colors, or by contrasting colors such as yellow standards and brown falls. Recently I found the most beautiful iris done in a petit-point chairseat. The iris were done in lovely soft blue purples and orchids against a soft eggshell background. It was so beautiful that it inspired me to get Mrs. Zeiser's Heirloom pattern Pastel and Iris just so I could copy this beautiful iris done in petit point. I am calling this the Rust Iris for identification only. I have used the same colors as were used for the open Wild Rose.

Falls:
1. First hook beards in a soft yellow, as shown in sketch #2 by Y.
2. Hook falls E and D with #6 for edging.
3. Hook #4 inside of #6.
4. If you desire, hook veinings as shown in sketch #2 with #6 or #5.
5. Hook #3 between veinings and in remaining spaces. We omitted #2 and #5 in sketch but you may add if you wish.

Standards:
1. On petal B hook #1 at tip and along edges for several rows as shown.
2. Hook #2 or #3 in center.
3. On petals A and C, hook #4 next to edging on section B.
4. Hook #3 next to #4 and along outer edges of petals as shown.
5. Hook #2 between #3.

Stem:
1. Hook stems in various shades of green, using shades of iris leaf. Separate the sections of the stem as shown in sketch #2 by using #4, #3, and #2 alternately.

SIX-PETAL TULIP

1. On petals B-C-D-E-F edge with the lightest shade #1 as shown in sketch #2.
2. Hook #6 or #6a in petals B and F at edging of D as shown.
3. On petals B and F hook #5 or #6 from base up through center, curving the line as shown, hook another shorter line along outer edge of B and F at base of petals.
4. Dovetail #4 between lines of #5.

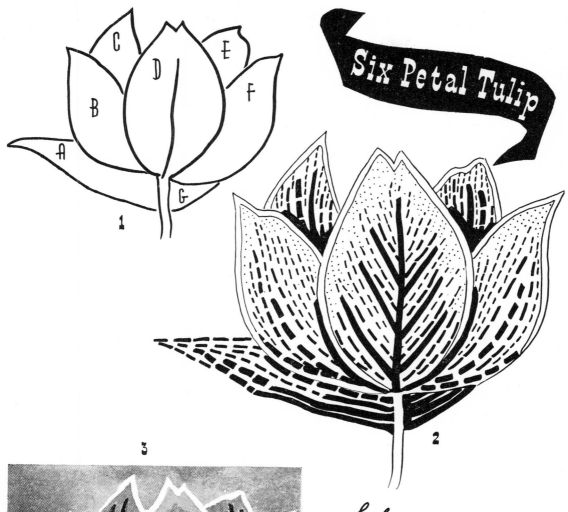

Six Petal Tulip

C
D
E
B
F
A
G

1

2

3

1 *Lightest* ──────
2 *Second Lightest* ············
3 *Medium Light* - - - - - -
4 *Medium Dark* ━ ━ ━ ━
5 *Second Darkest* ━━ ━━ ━━
6 *Darkest* ━━━━━━━

5. Dovetail #3 between #4, bringing lines nearer tips of petals.
6. Fill in the tips of petals with #2.
7. On petal G fill in completely with #6, the deepest shade.

Petals C and E:
  1. Hook #6 or #6a in the center and at base near edging of D-B-F.
  2. Hook #5 side of #6.
  3. Hook #4, dovetailing it in between #5 and #6.
  4. Dovetail #3 between #4 and #5.

Petal D:
  1. Hook center veining and side veinings of #6 or #6a (side veinings are not shown on pattern).
  2. Hook #4 next to side veining of #6.
  3. Hook #3 next to #4, bringing lines out farther to edge.
  4. Fill in spaces and tip with #2 as shown in sketch, bringing #2 almost all the way around edging and dovetailing it between other shades.

Petal A:
  1. Hook #6 or #6a and #5 at base and along edging of B.
  2. Hook #4 between #5 and #6.
  3. Fill tip of petal with #3 or #4.

Stem: Hook in a soft green—or yellow green.

SMALL TULIP

You may use the colors of the large tulip or wild rose.
  1. Edge each petal with #1 as shown in sketch.
  2. Hook #6 according to dark line on sketch in petals A and C, next to edging shade on petal D. Keep base of petals in darker shades.
  3. Hook #5 or #4 next to #6 on petals A and C.
  4. Hook #4 or #5 at base and outer lower edges of petals A and C as shown.
  5. Hook #4 or #3 in petals A and C alongside of #5 and up into petals.
  6. Fill in rest of petals with #2 or #3 shades, dovetailing in between the other shades near tip. Notice that petals A and C are not hooked exactly the same. You might enjoy trying your ideas and achieve an even better effect.

Petal D:
  1. Hook #6 in center veining, being sure to curve it slightly.

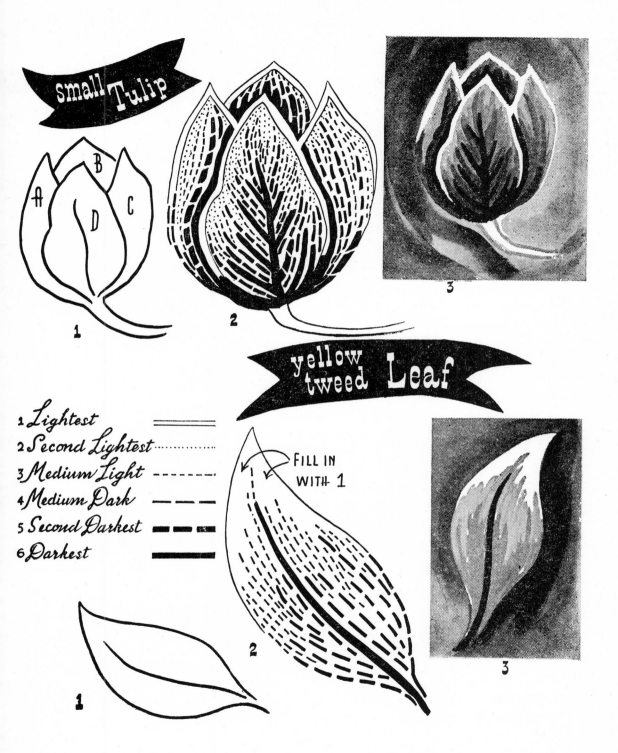

small Tulip

A   B
  D   C

1

2

3

yellow tweed Leaf

1 Lightest
2 Second Lightest
3 Medium Light
4 Medium Dark
5 Second Darkest
6 Darkest

FILL IN WITH 1

1

2

3

2. Hook #6 for side veinings if desired (these veinings are not shown in sketch #1).
3. Hook #5 and #6 at base of petal.
4. Working with the contour of side veining hook #4 or #5 next to #6.
5. Dovetail #3 between #4 or #5. Do not hook all the way out to the edge and vary the length of the lines.
6. Fill in spaces at top and along sides with #2, dovetailing between other shades as shown.

Petal B:
1. Hook #6 or #5 from base as shown in sketch.
2. Fill in between with #4.
3. Fill in at tip with #3.

YELLOW LEAVES

1. Vein leaf with #6. I used a dark rust.
2. Hook #4 on either side of the veining, fanning out the lines as you near the center of the leaf.
3. Hook #3, dovetailing it between #4 and fanning it out as you near the tip, as shown.
4. Tip the leaf with the #1 shade, dovetailing it down between #3.
   For these leaves I dyed some checked material in yellow dye, then added a bit of sky blue dye to get a more chartreuse shade. I removed a few pieces of material from the yellow dye before I added the blue.
5. Hook stems in a rust shade.

YELLOW AND BROWN IRIS

Falls:
1. Hook beards on falls E and D in a burnt orange as shown by O on color chart, facing page 62.
2. Although the veinings are not drawn in pattern you may hook them in if you desire. You may either hook dark veinings on light petals or light veinings on dark petals. I have hooked these veinings in with #6.
3. Hook #6 to edge falls E and D. (Use darker shades shown on right-hand side of O.)
4. Hook #5 next to #6 as shown.
5. Hook #4 next to #5.

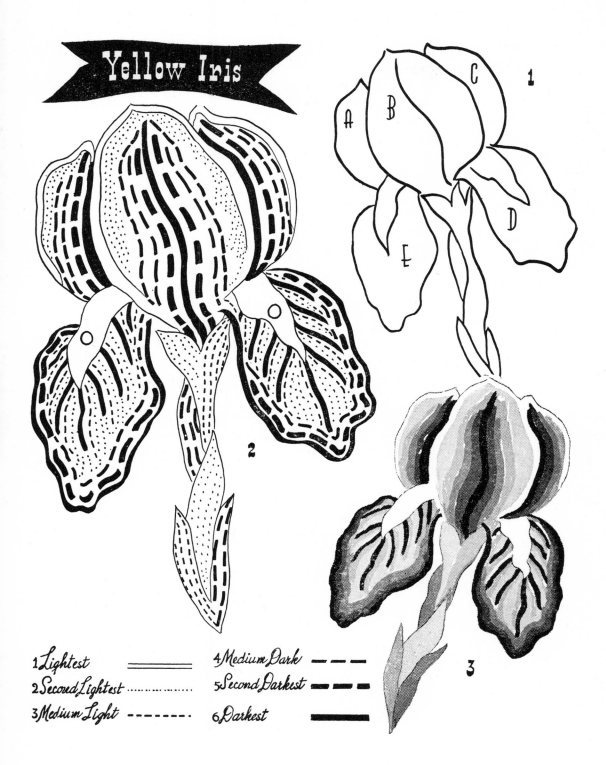

Yellow Iris

1 — A B C D E

2

3

1. Lightest ——————
2. Second Lightest ·················
3. Medium Light - - - - - - -
4. Medium Dark – – – –
5. Second Darkest ▬ ▬ ▬
6. Darkest ▬▬▬▬▬▬

6. Hook #3 and #2 next to veinings following contour of veinings. You may add the #4 if you wish.

7. Fill remaining spaces with #2. I have omitted using #1 but you may add it if you wish.

Standards: Use colors on left-hand side of O as shown on color chart.
1. Edge petal B with #1.
2. Hook #6 for center veining (curve line slightly).
3. Hook #5 either side of #6.
4. Hook #4 next to #5.
5. Omit #3 and hook #2 next to #4.
6. Fill remaining spaces with #2 as shown.

Petals A and C:
1. Hook #6 on petal A and C next to edging #1 on petal B.
2. Hook #5 next to #6.
3. Hook #4 next to #5.
4. Hook #2 in remaining spaces. Omit #3.

Stem:
1. Hook stems in various shades of green, using the shades of the iris leaf. Separate the sections of stem as shown in sketch by using #4, #3, and #2 alternately.

LARGE ROSEBUD

Using Rockwell's #4 swatch or yellow greens:
1. Hook #5 or #6 in section C at base of petal.
2. Hook #1 or lightest shade for edging in section A and B as shown.
3. Hook #4 from base of petal A and B, fanning lines out as shown.
4. Hook #3, dovetailing it in between #4.
5. Fill tip and remaining spaces with #2, dovetailing it between #3.
6. Hook #1 or #2 at the tip, which extends beyond the rosebud.

Rosebud (using some of the shades of red rose as shown on color plate):
1. Hook the circle at tip in #6, the darkest shade.
2. Hook #1 around the circle and follow contour of line down to base of bud as shown.
3. Hook #5 or #6 on left side of #1 as shown.

78

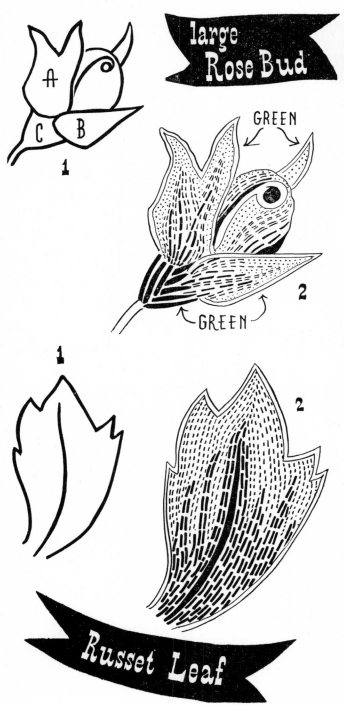

GREEN

GREEN

3

1

2

1

2

Russet Leaf

3

1 Lightest ═══════
2 Second Lightest ·········
3 Medium Light -------
4 Medium Dark — — —
5 Second Darkest
6 Darkest ▬▬▬▬▬

4. Hook #4 on left side next to #5.
5. Hook #3 or #2 in remaining spaces.
6. On right side of circle hook #2 next to shade #1 as shown.
7. Hook #3 shade next to #2.
8. Hook #4 next to #3.
9. Hook #5 or #6 at the very edge as shown.

NOTE: If you are unable to hook all six shades of red in this bud then choose one of the lighter shades, one of medium light and medium dark and then dark.

RUSSET LEAF

I call this Russet Leaf for identification only and am showing you only one section of leaf near large rose.

1. Hook the bright red rust veining or #6.
2. Edge leaf with #1 shade. You may also tip the leaf more by bringing this #1 shade down in between #3, if you prefer.
3. Hook #4 at base following contour of veining and fanning the lines as shown.
4. Dovetail #3 from tip of leaf between lines of #4.

NOTE: All leaves do not have to be made green. Your rug will be more interesting if you use, beside the lovely greens, many lovely plaids or tweeds, using colors, of course, that are in harmony with your other colors; but leaves may be gold, rust, browns, rose browns, etc. The veining of your leaves may be a very dark shade of the color used or it may be a contrasting color.

CUPPED TULIP

1. Edge all petals with #1 as shown in sketch.
2. Hook #6 or #6a on petal D for center veining. You may add to the side veinings if you desire; they are not drawn on pattern.
3. Hook #5 next to #6 on side veinings in petal D.
4. Hook #4 next to #5, varying the length of lines and do not bring all lines out to edge of D.
5. Dovetail #3 in remaining spaces as shown.
6. Hook #2 at tip (you may hook more of #2 instead of #3 if you wish).

80

1

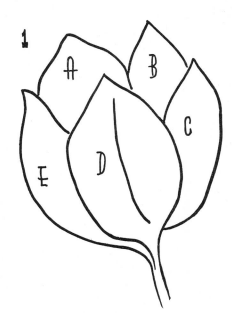

A B C E D

Cupped Tulip

2

3

1 *Lightest* ——————

2 *Second Lightest* ·················

3 *Medium Light* - - - - - - -

4 *Medium Dark* — — — — —

5 *Second Darkest* —– — –— —

6 *Darkest* ——————

Petals E and C:
1. Hook a veining of #6 or #6a or #5 in center of E and C, starting at base of petal and working up into center, curving lines as shown with the contour of petal.
2. Hook a line of #6 or #6a in E and C, next to edging of D.
3. Hook #5 either side of #6 (keep base of petal dark).
4. Hook #4, dovetailing between #5 and #6.
5. Fill tip with #2 or #3 as you prefer, dovetailing lines as shown between #4.

Petals A and B:
1. Hook #6 or #6a at base of petals as shown.
2. Hook a line of #6 up through center of petal as shown.
3. Hook #5 either side of #6.
4. Dovetail #4 between #5 and #6.
5. Dovetail #3 between #4 (omit if you do not have room).
6. Fill remaining space at tip with #2.

Stem: Hook in soft green or yellow green.

SMALL ROSEBUD

This small rosebud will take only about three shades of red, so from colors of large rose choose between #1, #1a, and #2, for light shades and #3 and #4 for medium shades, #5 and #6 for dark shades. It depends on whether you hook with very fine strips whether you can use three and four shades.

NOTE: Start with the greens (yellow green to bronze green, either iris green or rose leaf green).
1. Hook #5 at the base of bud G as shown in sketch, #2 (also in stem).
2. Hook #4 starting down where #5 is hooked and bring it up into center of parts D, E, F.
3. Hook #3 on either side of #4.
4. Hook #1 or #2 in tips of D, E, and F.
5. Hook #1 or #2 in A.

NOTE: Now hook reds (you may reverse this plan, using light shade at base and bringing the dark shade at tip).
1. Hook #1 or lightest shade you are using as shown in sketch to separate

82

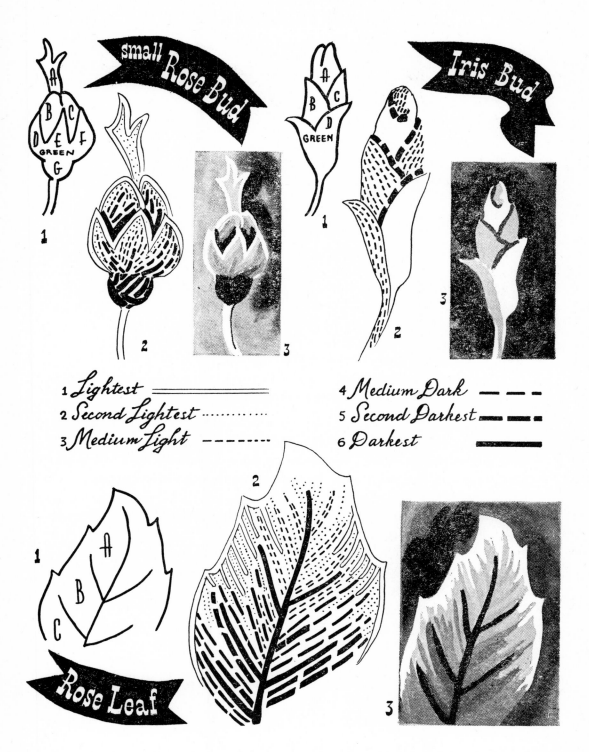

A B C F
D E
G
GREEN

small Rose Bud

1

2

3

A C
B D
GREEN

Iris Bud

1

2

3

1 Lightest ═══════
2 Second Lightest ············
3 Medium Light — — — —

4 Medium Dark — — — —
5 Second Darkest ▬ ▬ ▬
6 Darkest ▬▬▬▬▬

A
B
C

1

2

Rose Leaf

3

sections of bud. I would suggest you omit #2 if you do not have room for all four shades.

2. Hook #6 shade in base of B and C as shown.
3. Hook #4 shade up into center of bud.
4. Hook #3 or #2 as shown in sketch.

NOTE: Experiment with your own ideas and work out different ways of shading buds: Such little buds as these are fun for the novice to experiment with. Keep your scrapbook handy and hunt up ideas for rosebuds.

IRIS BUD

Use any of the shades you have used for your iris. We are using the rust shades.

1. Hook the base of the bud in the same greens as the rosebud, hooking one side with a #3 or #4 shade and the other side in #1 or #2 shade (section D).
2. Hook #5 or #6 of rust shades in B and C as shown in sketch.
3. Fill sections B and C with #3 or #4.
4. Fill section A with #1 (except at the tip).
5. Hook #5 at tip of bud according to the line in pattern.
6. Hook on the right side of this line #3 as shown.

ROSE LEAVES

NOTE: Although three shades of green, dark, intermediate, and light, will make this leaf, I prefer to use five or six shades. I have used here Rockwell's #4 yellow greens in some of the leaves and #7 Rockwell's forest greens for the other rose leaves. I have also added one lighter shade, making a total of six shades instead of just the five Rockwell shades. I like a much lighter shade for tipping.

If you observe the colored picture of the Easter Parade you will be able to see that I did not make any of the leaves exactly alike. Leaves are the easiest to experiment on for shading and you will have fun if you work out your own ideas. However, be very careful not to make the mistake that so many beginners do in shading a leaf—using a light green for a tip in section A and intermediate green for center section B and a dark green for base in section C, thus making a distinct division between the three shades. The skill of the hooker is evident by the way she shades a leaf or flower from light to dark, gradually or imperceptibly. Here is one advantage of using dyed material that is mottled. Always hook from center out to edge, following contour of veinings.

1. Hook center veining with a contrasting color such as rust or a harmonizing plaid as we have used, or hook veining in #6, of either Rockwell's #4 yellow greens or #7 forest greens.
2. Hook #5 at the base and next to #6 or side veinings. Keep the base of the leaf dark. Hook your line in different lengths; you will do a better job of shading if you do this. Also do not bring the darker shades out to the very edge (study sketch).
3. Dovetail #4 between #5 as in sketch.
4. In section B or center section hook #4 next to side veining.
5. Dovetail #3 between #4. Hook #2 in a few places. Be sure to vary the length of lines.
6. In section A hook #2 and #3 near veinings and as you near the tip hook only in #1 shade.
7. Bring #1 and #2 down along edge of leaf, bringing it into the spaces not hooked and dovetailing it between the other shades.

LARGE ROSE

NOTE: For such a large flower it is necessary to have at least six shades or more. I have used nine shades for the red rose, including black for the deepest shadow line. But so as not to confuse you and to carry out the key of six shades we have marked on the color plate of materials #1 or #1a, you may use either one or both.

1. Hook #1 or #1a along edges of all petals as shown in sketch. Notice on petals B, G, and K that there are tip-overs and these are to be filled in with either #1 or #1a. You may add #2 in K if you prefer as shown in one section of K. (Notice sketches 2 and 3.)
2. Using #5 or #6 (*not* #6a, which is black) hook a line directly under tip-over in B and G. Follow contour of tip-over.
3. Hook #6 or #6a for the center veining line, which runs from A along through base of B and up into C (see sketch 2). Also hook #6 or #6a for center veining in petals D-E-F-G.
4. You may hook a touch of yellow or yellow green just above B and down at base of J as I have done.
5. In J, which forms the cup of the rose, use all darker shades. Hook mostly

85

Center Rose

2

1 *Lightest* ────────

2 *Second Lightest* ············

3 *Medium Light* ── ── ── ──

4 *Medium Dark* ─ ─ ─ ─ ─

5 *Second Darkest* ═ ─ ═ ─ ═

6 *Darkest* ━━━━━━━━

1

K   K
J   J
H   A   K
        B   C
G   D
        F   E

Center
Rose

3

the deeper shades to give effect of depth and to make the rose cup for you. Hook #5 and #6 from base of J and hook lines in a curving effect, not straight; vary the length of lines up into K.

6. Hook a bit of #4 and #3 in J, dovetailing it between the deeper shades.

7. On petals B and G hook several lines of #6, starting at center and fanning out as shown, varying the lengths of the lines.

8. Hook #5 between #6 as shown.

9. Dovetail #4 between #5 and #6.

10. Hook remaining spaces with #2a or #3, dovetailing between #4 and #5.

11. Follow the above procedure for petals A-C-D-E-F-H, only add #2, and dovetail between #3.

XI. Cost and Care

Thought combined with deep feeling bestows a special
quality upon the work toward which it is directed. A gift
so made is transfused with a peculiar beauty and becomes
to the recipient a treasure without price.

—AMERICAN NEEDLEWORK

WHAT will it cost? Since it is a question the novice always asks, it
is of primary importance. It regulates and controls the purchase of
the so-called luxuries among which some may class our hobbies.
To me a hobby is not a luxury but a necessity, if for no other reason than
that a person with a hobby is seldom a lonely person. I must find in each day
some time I can call my own, to do with as I wish, some moments away from
everyday routine for creative thought and relaxation. I find this in hooked
rugs. Hooked rugs can be most inexpensively made. The woman with little
means may construct as beautiful a rug as the woman with plenty of money.

The beautiful hooked rug, in effect, comes out of the woman's creative ability, not out of her pocketbook. There is, of course, some cost, for nothing, even beauty, is procured for no consideration whatever. It is possible, however, to make hooked rugs from scraps that accumulate in the course of years of normal living. But these rugs are seldom beautiful. Too much sheer chance goes into their construction. They are not planned, because the rag bag is not planned. Though the rag bag has been years in the filling, the many beautiful shades needed to make a lovely rug simply will not be found it it. You have to find materials where you can, paying as little for them as possible. To most of us, hunting for materials is part of the fun. It is like window-shopping and counter-searching—the delight of all women.

The true shopper, given time, will find what she seeks and give herself the enjoyment as well. The hunt for color is much of the sheer joy of creating. While searching for one shade, I encounter many hues, many colored tweeds and plaids, which at the moment I do not need, but I know how lovely each will look in some future scroll or design. I try to look ahead in my planning, buttressing in advance future rugs for which I may never find these same lovely materials again. The person who hunts and sees only materials for current rugs makes progress, but never as much as the artist who continues building. I have a large collection of colors, plaids, and mixtures. They are my rugmaking gold mine. And I continue to buy!

Most material today costs over fifty cents a pound. I would not advise anyone to buy material by the yard; it is much too expensive. There are dealers in the business of furnishing new woolen materials for hooking rugs. (See back of book for information.)

At this writing one of the rugs pictured herein can be made for about $15. This cost rises and falls with time, naturally. It can also be regulated by whether everything is purchased, ready-made swatches are used, or whether you dye old materials. The carefully hooked rug that costs about $15 to make can be sold for several hundred dollars. This may seem quite high in price, but hundreds of hours go into the hooking of the rug and even though it is a hobby job, time so spent should be paid for if sold. There are some hookers who would not sell their rugs at any price; they have put too much of themselves into their product. These are the heirlooms of tomorrow. These artists are also aware that they are dotting their floors with rugs more valuable than any budget would allow them to purchase at today's high price of commercial carpeting. The cost of lovely hooked rugs is the total of materials and lessons, your time is your own.

COST AND CARE

Will the rug wear well and how do you clean it?

If the rug is hooked on a fine grade of imported burlap, with a fine hook, and with finely cut strips of wool hooked into almost every mesh of the burlap according to weight of material; if it is not packed, and hooked evenly with a low pile; if the ends drawn through are clipped even with the loops; the rug will last for years without showing signs of wear. *Remember that loops are not clipped*. The result is firm, even nap.

A rug should always be rolled with the right side on top or on the outside because you have the nap on the outside, and folding it or rolling it with the top inside tends to break the burlap backing. Never fold a rug.

To clean a rug, start with a thorough vacuuming, which should remove the dirt. Then if you wish to shampoo the rug to restore or brighten the colors, use a good commercial shampoo. Use about a quart of suds and a small vegetable brush or sponge. Apply the suds to a small portion of the rug at a time, working rather quickly. Do not get the rug so wet that it penetrates to the burlap. Brush foam over and off rug *fast*. Work on a small area at a time, then go over that same spot with a soft cloth wrung out of clear water to absorb all suds. When you have finished shampooing the rug, let it remain flat several hours to dry. Never put these beautiful rugs in a washing machine.

When you finish hooking a rug you should press it. This generally improves the rug and will make it lie flat. Wet a heavy pressing cloth, wring it out, lay it on the wrong side of the rug, use a hot iron to steam the rug. Turn the rug over. Use press cloth or towel, steam right side *lightly,* leave rug flat for several hours to dry thoroughly.

Do *not* allow water to penetrate to burlap.

91

XII. Dyeing Is Fun

And it may be that all which lends
The soul an upward impulse here,
With a diviner beauty blends,
And greets us in a holier sphere.

—John Greenleaf Whittier

TO MANY of the more experienced hookers dyeing is not only an art but it is as much fun as the actual hooking of a rug. There really is no such thing as failure. Even if results are not what one had hoped for, dyed material will always find a place sooner or later. So often women shy away from the dyeing experiences because sometime or other they have tried to dye a garment and have had poor results. The dyeing was uneven or blotchy and the dress or garment believed spoiled. As a result, many women have no desire to try their hand at dyeing for rugs. However, this very uneven coloring, this happenstance mixture may be exactly what the hooker needs or is looking for. Often these very uneven effects will achieve lovelier and more beautiful scrolls, leaves, or flowers than any plain material could ever do. So do not think that because you cannot dye evenly you are spoiling anything. Once you start you will find that dyeing is really fun!

Our pioneer ancestors had little or nothing in the way of materials or dyes with which to work. Lack, however, did not dampen their enthusiasm or allay their yearning for beauty. Dyes were a mystery to them and they solved it by experimentation supplemented by what they could learn from the Indians. Dyes may be a mystery to us at first but they need not be for very long. Only half a century ago commercial dyes were still difficult for some housewives to obtain and so they turned to the same sources for dyes as did their ancestors. My own mother has often told me how she helped Grandma hook rugs during long winter evenings, also how she helped tend and sheer the sheep, wash and card the wool, spin and weave it into cloth. Grandma, like her forebears, often scoured the woods for bark and roots of certain trees; blossoms, leaves, and berries, in order to obtain the dye she needed for her wools. Their color range was obviously restricted to what the immediate locality provided. Some dyes came from Germany but they were, generally, difficult to obtain. Brown was obtained from the hemlock tree bark, from juniper, and from walnut trees; blue from the indigo plant; yellow from onion skins and alder blossoms. By combining blue and yellow Grandma obtained green. Red beets and cranberries produced a red. Many wild berries, such as cherries, grapes, and blueberries were also used. Colors were made "fast" with the use of alum and salt.

Some maple bark produces a rose tan, some a light brown. Birch bark produces a yellow, coffee beans a dark yellow tan, goldenrod flowers a yellow brown, dahlia an orange, madder a red, and tea leaves a rose tan. These were natural dyes and were clear and bright but never harsh, so that many of the bright colors could be used together. Today's dyes are synthetic and are purer and are sharp and more difficult to use together. Natural dyes contain impurities that help to soften the colors.

Many early experiments of the pioneer housewife, performed in the evening when her chores were done, provided her with interesting diversion from the dull routine of the day. These experiments were carefully recorded and handed down from generation to generation. Records of dyes, which the early pioneer produced, were exchanged with distant neighbors during rare visits. Later, rugging parties were enjoyed as a means of exchanging patterns and dyes.

It is difficult for us today to visualize the obstacles our ancestors had to overcome to provide us with a heritage of hooked rugs, an art all its own. But we are more fortunate to have a wide selection of colors from which to pick and choose our dyes. These commercial dyes are offered us by Cushing Perfection Dye Company of Dover-Foxcroft, Maine. They are widely recommended by many experts and experienced teachers because they offer not only a wide selection of colors, but a good quality in the colors, and a fast dye.

I feel that you should have some knowledge of dyeing even though you may be so fortunate as to have a large supply of wool on hand or may be able to obtain what you need from wool supply houses or mills. It is not necessary to dye to obtain a beautiful hooked rug, but you will find that you collect a good many colors that need to be dipped in a dye bath to make them lovelier for your rug. Dyed materials often lend more striking effects than the original colors could ever have done. Then, too, it is necessary for many women who live far away from wool centers to dye in order to obtain any of the many shades and tints they will need.

Please bear in mind that instructions given here are for the novice who has never tried to dye; they will initiate her into an interesting adventure. If the reader wishes to delve into the subject more fully she will find excellent printed material through Cushing Perfection Dye Company, mentioned above.

Equipment Needed for Dyeing

A small enamel dish or pail, a 4-quart size for about a pound of wool.

A larger pan for rinsing (or use the kitchen sink).

A wooden stick or poker to lift the dyed materials from the boiling water.

Enamel or glass cups or jars.

A pair of rubber gloves, if desired.

A bag of pure salt, not iodized.

Bleach water to remove stains on sink and utensils.

Woolen materials.

Used garments, torn and cleaned before dyeing.

Plurosol, for soaking materials so that they dye easier.

Notebook, to keep records.

Make sure that all used garments are ripped and cleaned before dyeing. Don't use worn-out materials; it is a waste of time to hook worn-out materials into a lovely rug that one wishes to last a lifetime. However, wool skirts, shirts, dresses, coats, bathrobes, still in good condition, in both plain, tweed, or plaid, offer a wealth of dyeing materials. Many of your friends and neighbors will shower you with such gifts when they learn that you are hooking and dyeing—until they themselves become interested in the art of hooking. Then father will need to take stock of his wardrobe, for many a hooker has snitched an old sport coat or trousers while Dad was blissfully ignorant of the fact until he needed one or the other and forced Mother to confess. This could be one of the reasons why Dad becomes interested in hooking rugs—to make sure his clothes aren't being cut into rags! Old white flannels have a way of disappearing and ending up on a clothesline, dyed a lovely shade of rose or blue. Remember also that there are materials to which chemicals have been added to make them waterproof. Cushing solves this problem with Plurosol, a special detergent preparation for "wetting out" all textile materials, wool especially, in preparation for dyeing.

Experimenting, keeping records, files, scrapbooks are "musts." Dabbling is definitely encouraged, especially if you are one who enjoyed the mudpie-making urge, or had a sublime curiosity to mess into everything. This early effort at self-expression may pay dividends in dyeing results. You can be serious and have fun, too. Records should be carefully kept, even when there is more fun than seriousness. First mistakes do not matter, for great knowledge has grown from errors, in dyeing as in every human activity. Dyeing may not be for you if you cannot follow instructions. It is discouraging to teacher and pupils alike when dyed materials do not remain colorfast, or fade out quickly in the rug. By using a commercial dye that you know will remain fast, like Cushing's, and following directions as to time material must stay in the dye bath, you need not fear that your colors will not hold.

A huge container or large quantities of boiling water are not needed for successful dyeing as many beginners appear to believe. It is easier to use a small container, two-quart or four-quart size. This size saves trouble, reduces the problem to manageable size, and lessens possible confusion for the novice; it automatically limits the quantity of material to be dyed. One important advantage of a small amount of material in small amounts of dye in a small container is that if there is waste it will be negligible, both in time and materials. You work slowly until you have acquired the knack of dyeing and a liking for the adventure. Nothing is ever really spoiled, for the dyed piece can be put into another dye pot and the color changed, or the color can be removed and you can start again.

A pupil of mine who has always had good results in her dyeing, keeps a box of materials on hand, some of which may not be good for anything, such as dirty-colored blues or grays, or many neutral shades, or plaids and pastels that may contain a lot of white, assorted pieces of nondescript material. Whenever she plans to dye for a certain color she includes some of those varicolored items in the dye bath, keeping a careful record of their original color, the color in which they are being dipped, adding to the record the color resulting from dyeing. Many of these pieces go into different dye baths, so she knows just what her odds and ends will produce in the way of new colors. This record is her reference file. You will soon discover that such a file is virtually indispensable. The record need not be a chore but a fascinating record of your progress. You should exercise care in adding differently colored pieces to dye baths, however, for strong colors, such as red, or the dark colors, may spoil the color in the bath. Remember that different weaves of the same color will dye differently. You should study the chapter on color and the color wheel so that you will be better equipped to understand how dyed colored materials become new and different.

It is a good idea to keep white flannel coats and trousers for dyeing the lighter shades of flowers. Other materials may be used for dyeing the darker colors. White is often difficult to obtain so it should be saved to use in dyeing tints or lighter shades. Old homespun blankets are priceless treasures, but if you are going to cut up one why not save it for background material?

Many of the flowers or scrolls you will hook will require anywhere from five to eight shades, perhaps more. Five gradations of shades or tints are easily procurable. Mahogany dye can be worked down into five to eight gradations of shades or tints for the scroll in the Easter Parade. Chartreuse used for a veining with this will produce a lovely effect. Remember that there are many different methods of dyeing to get different results. Each teacher has her way of doing it. My best advice is to make a start, then follow the method best liked. If you wish to dye material evenly do not crowd it into the container. Just be sure that it is covered and that the dye reaches all parts of it. If an uneven dyeing is desired, then crowd plenty of material into the container, so that some material will absorb more dye than other material. Material crowded into the dye bath should be left longer to make sure the dye is fast. Color deepens with time in the bath. Try putting some plain boiling water in another container beside the dye bath, then transfer some of the top pieces in the dye bath to the boiling water. Add salt and leave the material in the boiling water for the required time. The result will be lighter shades from the boiling water than from the dye bath.

In rinsing remember to change the temperature of the water gradually so that woolens will not be shrunk. In dyeing all-wool fabrics, the use of vinegar on the basis of one cupful to the pound of goods, in the dye bath in the place of, or in addition to salt, will give a more complete "exhaust" of the dye. A little Plurosol in the final rinse water will leave the goods soft and pliable.

Some packages of dye contain a large amount of dye, because some dyes are easier for manufacturers to obtain than others. This difference makes it difficult to give exact directions. All packages contain enough dye to do one pound of material, so we'll go by that, though packages contain "more or less" than a tablespoon of dye.

First, tear the material into the size strips desired. Divide these strips into the number of different shades required.

1. Dissolve one package of dye in two cups of boiling water to make the dye solution. Stir until dissolved.
2. Have dye pot on stove containing three quarts of warm water. This is the dye bath.
3. Add 1½ teaspoons, or ½ tablespoon, of dye solution to the dye bath.
4. Add material, which has been soaked in water and squeezed out, to the dye bath containing the 1½ teaspoons (or ½ tablespoon) of dye solution. This will give you your lightest shade.
5. After ten minutes add a handful of salt and let simmer for twenty minutes.
6. Remove with poker and rinse first in hot water, then gradually change temperature of next two rinse waters. Stretch material and hang out to dry.
7. Use same dye bath, add 1 tablespoon of dye solution to dye bath. Repeat steps 4-5-6 for second shade.
8. For third shade, still using same dye bath, add the next amount of dye solution, which is 2 tablespoons. Repeat steps 4-5-6.
9. For fourth shade, using same dye bath as above, increase dye solution to 4 tablespoons and add to dye bath. Repeat steps 4-5-6.
10. For fifth shade, still using same dye bath, add 8 tablespoons of dye solution (or ½ cup) to dye bath. Repeat steps 4-5-6. Add water if necessary.
11. For sixth shade still using same dye bath, add 16 tablespoons (or one cup) dye solution. Repeat steps 4-5-6. Add water if necessary.

If you wish to dye only about a quarter pound of material it would waste dye to use a whole package. The following method is suggested, especially for strong or dark colors, using only a little dye. A quarter pound of material should give you twelve strips of material, 4″ x 9″.

1. Dissolve ¼ teaspoon of dye in 1 cup boiling water. This is the dye solution.
2. Place dyeing utensil containing three cups of warm water on stove. This is the dye bath.
3. Add to the dye bath ½ tablespoon of dye solution. This will be the lightest shade.
4. Place a number of strips of wet material in the dye bath.
5. Simmer for 10 minutes, then add 2 tablespoons salt.
6. Simmer for an additional 15 minutes.
7. Remove pieces of dyed material with poker, rinse several times.
8. Hang material out to dry, stretching it so it will cut easier.
9. Continue as above with rest of material, each time doubling the amount of dye solution in the dye bath as follows: (Add salt each time and leave material in bath for required time).
10. Use 1 tablespoon dye in same dye bath. Repeat steps 4-5-6-7-8.
11. Use 2 tablespoons in same dye bath, repeat steps 4-5-6-7-8.
12. Use 4 tablespoons in same dye bath, repeat steps 4-5-6-7-8.
13. Use 8 tablespoons in same dye bath, repeat steps 4-5-6-7-8.

Now if you have a blanket or other light material for a background, don't ruin it by pushing the whole thing into a bath of dark dye. If you wish to tint it use a very small amount of dye to dye bath. A tint of Cushing's Perfection Dye, Mahogany, becomes a lovely rose tan if carefully worked out. Always test, if you have no record or advice, and are a beginner, with a small bit of cloth in the dye bath. It is easier to change the dye than to remove a darker color from dyed goods. Cushing's Perfection Seal Brown, Wine, Burgundy, Black, or Navy are good for backgrounds. Old Ivory, Champagne, Ecru, or a tint of Mahogany or Seal Brown are good for light backgrounds.

Many rug-artists like their backgrounds mottled. If this appeals to you, make a dye bath of, let us say, tint of Cushing's Perfection Dye, Seal Brown, and place material in dye bath, dabble a little of the dye solution of Seal Brown over the material. As the dye hits certain spots these will be darker, other areas remaining very near original color. Turn the material over and repeat. Remember, as above, to test the dye bath, and the process suggested here, first with small pieces of cloth to avoid waste.

DYEING IS FUN

Dry dyeing may also be practiced as you make progress. Using a *small amount of water* in the dye pot, you make steam do the job of the boiling water. The water must be boiling very hard, with the material protruding well above the water. Sprinkle dry dye very sparingly over the exposed parts of the material. The steam will help dissolve this dry dye. To experiment further—always keeping records!—poke the material into the water once or twice. After material has been in the water about five minutes add salt and, if you wish you may then add another color dye, being sure to sprinkle dry dye sparingly where other dye did not touch. This is an excellent way to dye for autumn leaves.

If you wish to change the color of your material, you may try some of the following suggestions:

COLOR OF MATERIAL		DYE TO USE		RESULT
Red	+	Blue	=	Purple
Red	+	Yellow	=	Scarlet
Red	+	Purple	=	Red Purple
Red	+	Orange	=	Light Red
Blue	+	Yellow	=	Green
Blue	+	Orange	=	Dull Gray
Blue	+	Pink	=	Lavender (if Blue is light)
Yellow	+	Red	=	Scarlet
Yellow	+	Green	=	Light Green
Yellow	+	Orange	=	Yellow Orange
Yellow	+	Pink	=	Shell Pink
Green	+	Red	=	Black
Green	+	Yellow	=	Light Green
Green	+	Blue	=	Greenish Blue
Purple	+	Blue	=	Bluish Purple
Purple	+	Yellow	=	Greenish Brown
Purple	+	Brown	=	Reddish Brown
Purple	+	Red	=	Reddish Purple

So hasten, dear readers,
To the joys of hooking,
And if you wish revealed
The secrets of the color wheel,
Then gather your dyes and your wools
And see what magic you will brew
When in the pot you stir
A bit of red, now add some blue,
And lo!
You've neither red nor blue,
But a lovely purple hue.

—V. B. U.

Every experience deeply felt in life needs to be passed along,
whether it be through words or music, chiseled in stone,
painted with a brush or sewn with a needle. It is a way of
reaching for immortality.

—AMERICAN NEEDLEWORK

Dreams

Tonight with hook in hand
My fingers swiftly glide
Across the burlap taut and wide;
I hook my dreams into a new design.

You whom I long have loved
Beside me there
Deeply engrossed in a book;
And as I hook I wonder—
Are you on a trip to Mars?
Or fighting with Custer?

And at my feet
Stretched out
Are you my son,
Placing some foreign stamps
In a book.
And are you wondering
What it would be like
To visit China or Calcutta?

And then you turn
And looking up, ask,
What are you dreaming about, Mum?
Laughing at you
I answer:

See this blue I am hooking in my rug?
I snatched it from the sky
In sunny Italy
As we flew by.

These browns and golds and russet shades
I worked into my scroll
Are tints which autumn lavishly bestowed
Upon our fair New England shores.

This deep and lovely red
I took from off the cranberry bog
On beautiful Cape Cod.

This rose I hooked
With petals cupped
A maiden fair
Plucked from her hair
On the beach at Waikiki.

These lovely greens
I hooked into my leaves
Are the jewels rare
I found everywhere.

Dreaming? Ah, yes, my son;
But let us not forget
In searching far
For greater worlds to conquer
That very close to home
The real joys are.

      —V.B.U.

Where to Obtain Supplies for Hooking Rugs

RUG PATTERNS:

Louise Hunter Zeiser
54 Irving Ave.
Providence, R.I.

Mrs. Clyde Mackenzie
33 Arnold St.
Providence, R.I.

Mrs. Royal Manson
18 Church St.
Hudson, Mass.

Mrs. Helen Carlson
Merrimac, N.H.

Mrs. Charlotte Stratton
68 Haywood St.
Greenfield, Mass.

Cushing Perfection Dye Co.
Dover-Foxcroft, Maine

CUTTING MACHINES:

Mr. Harry Fraser
17 Spring St.
Manchester, Conn. (Bliss)

Mr. Howard Burdwood
So. Portland, Maine (Rigby)

L. H. Gibbs
Clinton, Mass.

SWATCHES:

Mrs. Lillian Stoliker
14 Kenilworth Rd.
Shrewsbury, Mass.

Mrs. Clarisse Cox
9141 East Arcadia Ave.
San Gabriel, California (wholesale only)

Hook-Art Guild
P.O. Box 57
Cumberland Mills, Maine

Rockwell Studios
Shreveport, Louisiana

Mrs. Eleanor Hambrecht
112 Stetson Ave.
Swampscott, Mass.

Mrs. E. J. Whitten
61 Long Beach Rd.
York Beach, Maine

FRAMES:

Mr. Harry Fraser
17 Spring St.
Manchester, Conn.

Mr. George Forsey
22 Ruggles St.
Westboro, Mass.

Mr. Harold Martin
Box 244
Greenville, R.I.

WOOL MATERIAL:

Berry Paper Stock Co.
Taunton, Mass.

Natick Mill Outlet
64A North Maine St.
Natick, Mass.

Berkowitz Wool Stock
Second St.
Chelsea, Mass.

Hook Art Guild
P.O. Box 57
Cumberland Mills, Maine

Mrs. E. J. Whitten
61 Long Beach Rd.
York Beach, Maine

DYE:

Cushing Perfection Dye
Dover-Foxcroft, Maine

RUG-LITE:

Wilder Rug-Hooking Supply Co.
12 Brantwood Rd.
Worcester, Mass.

WISS SHEARS:

Mrs. Alice Martin
Box 244
Greenville, R.I.

DYE MANUAL:

ANYONE CAN DYE—by Clarisse Cox
Cushing Perfection Dye
Dover-Foxcroft, Maine

"SWATCHETTES" by Clarisse Cox

These miniature swatches are numbered to correspond with the formulas in the book. $3.50 a set. Obtain from Cushing Perfection Dye or order from Clarisse C. Cox.

Heirloom Rug Patterns

Obtainable from Louise Hunter Zeiser, 54 Irving Avenue, Providence, R. I.

#500—Caswell Hearth 22¼″ x 60″ $5.25.
Section of famous Caswell carpet. Center motive—basket of grapes, flowers, and Japanese lanterns. Sawtooth border. Kent II, plate 187, page 162.

#501—Sheraton 26″ x 42″ $3.75.
Repeat medallions containing floral motives.

#501A—Sheraton 38″ x 66″ $6.50.
Same as #501.

#502—Pansy 34½″ x 44″ $4.00.
Border and center medallion—massed pansies.

#503—Coral Gardens 30″ x 54″ $5.00.
Colorful underwater scene with coral and coral fish. Border of shells.

#504—Pine and Berries 32″ x 81″ $8.00.
Leafy scroll. Center of pine with cones, alder berries, barberry, mistletoe, and holly.

#505—Roumanian Convent 48″ x 83″ $11.50.
Ornate acanthus scroll surrounding wreath of bell-flowers. Center—roses and buds.

#506—Paisley Shawl 68″ x 98½″ $25.00.
Copy of handsome antique Paisley shawl.

#507—Rockweed Border 72″ x 96″ (6′ x 8′) $25.00.
Unusual border of rockweed with a myriad of small flowers and buds. Floral center. Kent I, plate 58, page 62.

#508—Clipper 32″ x 50″ $4.50.
Clipper ship under full sail.

#509—Queen Anne 28½″ x 46½″ $4.00.
Banded medallion motives alternating with English woodcut rose. Kent I, plate 39, page 41.

#509A—Queen Anne 37¾″ x 64½″ $6.50.
Same as #509.

#510—Diamond Bordered Oval 72″ x 84″ (6′ x 7′) $20.00.
Center of mixed flowers in an oval of plume leaves. Narrow band of leaves around outer edge. Diamond motives fill area between plumes and outer leaf border. Kent I, plate 52, page 55.

#511—Acanthus Border 60″ x 92″ (5′ x 7′8″) $20.00
Graceful acanthus scroll. Floral center.

#512—Triple Scalloped Feathers 35″ x 120″ $13.00.
Unique feathery scroll with three floral spray motives.

#512A—Double Scalloped Feathers 35″ x 92″ $11.00.

#513—Chestnut Leaf Border 48″ x 86″ $10.00.
Old-fashioned geometric, framed with broad chestnut leaf border.

#514—Stepped Medallions 54″ x 94″ $13.50.
Unusual geometric—diagonals formed by overlapping blocks. Kent I, plate 44, page 43.

#514A—Stepped Medallions 34″ x 54″ $5.00.

#515—Mille Fleurs 84″ x 108″ (7′ x 9′) $30.00.
Same border as #507. Heavy inner floral wreath around small floral center.

#516—White Oak 72″ x 108″ (6′ x 9′) $27.50.
Handsome interlacing oak leaf and acorn tracery design, framed with oak leaf border.

#517—Aubusson Antique 108″ x 144″ (9′ x 12′) $50.00.
Copy of very old French carpet. Graceful flowing scrolls and flowers.

#518—Little Boy Blue 36″ x 50″ $5.00.
Familiar nursery character asleep by haystack. Landscape background. Poppy-daisy border. Companion to #519.

#519—Little Bo Peep 36″ x 50″ $5.00.
The well-known nursery character with appropriate landscape. Companion to #518.

#520—Panel Center 27″ x 54″ $4.75.
Geometric border. Field-mixed flowers.

#520A—Panel Center (double panel) 27″ x 90″ $8.00.

#520B—Panel Center (triple panel) 27″ x 132″ $11.50.

#521—Peterborough Antique 79″ x 118″ (6′7″ x 9′10″) $35.00.
Large shell scrolls. Inner fine scroll oval. Floral corners and floral center.

#522—Wide Oriental 50″ x 59″ $9.50.
Copy of very old carpet.

#523—Home to Thanksgiving 30″ x 47″ $4.50.
Copy of old Currier & Ives print.

#524—Verbenas 31″ x 51″ $4.75.
Graceful scroll surrounding needlepoint center of roses and verbenas.

#525—Riviera 52″ x 87″ $13.50.
Mixed flower center, surrounded by wreath of scrolls which in turn is surrounded by oval band of flowers. Floral corners. Can be hooked oblong or oval.

#526—Nova Scotia 24½″ x 33″ $3.00.
Country village winter scene with horse and sleigh.

#527—Barrington 40″ x 73″ $8.00.
Leafy scroll border framing end clusters of grapes and mixed floral center.

#528—Shirley Poppies 45″ x 80″ $11.00.
Mixed flower center, poppies predominating. Border of scrolls and poppies.

#529—Grandma Hastings 23″ x 40″ $3.00.
Copy of unusual antique. Center—graceful spray of mixed leaves. Border of similar leaves with a few rosebuds.

#530—New Hampshire Antique 42″ x 81″ $10.00.
Copy of an extraordinarily fine old rug. A rather intricate scroll frames a large oval center of mixed flowers.

#531—All-over Stair Carpet 27″ wide $2.75 per yd.
Stunning all-over conventional design.

#532—Velvet Flowers 37″ x 65″ $6.50.
Mixed floral center. Floral scroll border with sprays of velvet flowers.

#533—Amber Grain 43¼″ x 70¼″ $9.00.
Large graceful bouquet of roses, poppies, cornflowers, morning-glories, and wheat. Border of leaves and wheat.

#534—National Bouquet 37″ x 62″ $6.25.
The forty-eight State flowers gracefully combined in one large bouquet.

#535—Flower Bells 35½″ x 60″ $6.00.
Center—trumpet flowers, poppies, lilies, morning-glories, Canterbury bells, crocuses, iris, tulips. Border—double-edge leaf scroll with cup-shaped poppies.

#536—Minuet 36″ x 60½″ $6.00.
Center—sprays of single roses and leaves with sprays of star flowers, bell flowers and fuchsias. Border—single roses and buds with ribbon and bow knots.

#537—Easter Parade 37″ x 64″ $6.50.
Companion to #538. Center—one large rose, single

roses, tulips, iris, and star flowers. Leaf scrolls form oval around center. Roses and buds in corners. Can be hooked oblong or oval.

#538—Summer Promenade 37″ x 64″ $6.50.
Companion to #537. Center—one large rose, lilies, balloon flowers, nasturtiums, black-eyed Susans and petunias. Long plume leaf motives which interlock form oval around the center. Petunias and buds in corners. Can be hooked oblong or oval.

#539—Lilac Time 33″ x 46″ $4.50.
Medallion center with roses, tulips, and lilacs. A compound leaf scroll forms the border.

#540—Gaillardia 29″ x 52″ $4.75.
Center—peony surrounded by gaillardias, black-eyed Susans, tulips, roses, snowdrops, and four-o'clocks. Simple scroll border. Gaillardia in each corner.

#541—Bonnie Brae 29″ x 46″ $4.25.
Center—tulip flowers and buds, columbine and bell flowers. Border—tulip flowers and ivy leaves.

#542—Hollyhocks 26½″ x 38″ $3.00.
Center—three hollyhocks, buds and leaves surrounded by cosmos and phlox. Simple scroll border.

#543—Heartsease 30″ x 51″ $4.75.
Center—single rose, morning-glories and pansies. Broad veined scroll with exaggerated veinings.

#544—Lillibet 30″ x 51″ $4.75.
Center—wild roses, strawberries, Star of Bethlehem, mimosa and scilla. Seahorse scroll forms oval around center. Mimosa and scilla in corners. Can be hooked oblong or oval.

#545—Fruit Medley 30″ x 51″ $4.75.
Companion to #546. Graceful scrolls suitable for two-color combinations. Center—two large peonies, flanked by helianthus. Grape cluster at each end. Plum, peach, cherry, pear.

#546—Flower Medley 30″ x 51″ $4.75.
Companion to #545. Same scroll. Center—two large roses, daffodils, iris, snowdrops, morning-glories, bleeding hearts, tulips.

#547—Simplicity 26″ x 38″ $3.00.
Beginner's rug. Center—two roses, morning-glories, and bell flowers. Long simple leaf scrolls.

#548—Block Prints 43″ x 75″ $7.50.
8″ blocks of alternating hit-and-miss and flower motives. All flowers different.

#548A—Block Prints 27″ x 43″ $3.50.
Same as #548.

#548B—Block Prints 27″ x 43″ $3.50.
Same as #548—flower motives differ from those of #548A.

#548D—Block Prints. 8′8″ x 12′ $47.50.
Same as #548. This size is printed with extra burlap which will allow a 4″ border on all four sides. No two flower motives alike.

#548E—Block Prints 7′4″ x 8′8″ $30.00.
Same as #548D.

#549—Snow White 33″ x 54″ $5.00.
Center—poppy, tulips, narcissus, phlox. Inch-wide scroll border coils gracefully in corners.

#550—Trellis 27″ x 7′7½″ (27″ x 91½″) $8.00.
Running border of trumpet flowers and buds. Diagonal lines form a lattice background through the center.

#550A—Trellis 27″ x 10′ (27″ x 120″) $10.50.
Same as #550.

#550B—Trellis 27″ x 12′4½″ $12.50.
Same as #550.

#550C—Trellis Stair Carpet 27″ wide $2.75 per yd.
Same as #550. Stocked in 2 yd. and 2¾ yd. lengths.

#550M—Trellis 27″ x 36″ $3.00.
Same as #550.

#551—Melody 37″ x 65½″ $6.50.
Center—two roses, poppy, daffodils, morning-glories, calythorix, marianthus, and Australian cranberry. Leaf scroll border.

#552—Queensland 38″ x 43½″ Oval $4.25.
Center—two roses and dahlia with poppies, morning-glories, tulips, Canterbury bells. Border—a series of small C scrolls, each ending in a three-leaf motive. Companion scroll to #562.

#553—Ocean Swell 27″ x 37″ $3.00.
Center—double rose, wild rose, dahlia, iris, Johnny-jump-ups, daisies, day-lilies. Small scrolls—like ocean swells.

#554—Andover Antique 37″ Round $4.00.
Simple pattern of four flower clusters (single rose, poppy, lily) alternating with four C scrolls. Plain center. Copy of an old rug.

#555—Pansy Antique 38″ x 73″ $7.50.
Leaves and stems form border and are scattered through center. Three large pansies in center of rug. Another group of three pansies near each end. Copy of an old rug.

#556—Abigail's Parlor 36″ x 63″ $6.50.
Center—three roses, rosebuds and tulip flowers. Circular scrolls in corners with tulip flowers terminating the scrolls.

#557—Museum Antique 38″ x 72″ $7.50.
Center—mostly sprays of flower buds and leaves with one large rose. Unusual leaf scrolls with heavy midvein. Copy of an old rug.

#558—Early Threshold 25½″ x 37″ Half Round $3.00.
Center—roses and rosebuds in bush form. Scroll formed of variegated leaves. Copy of an old rug.

#559—Shalimar 46″ x 88″ $12.00.
Elaborate center with roses, buds, hibiscus, tulips, morning-glories, trumpet flowers, nasturtiums, poppies, zinnias, lilies, snowdrops. Scroll border.

#560—Rose of Sharon 33″ x 55″ $5.00.
Semi-conventional 11-inch blocks of traditional Rose of Sharon quilt pattern, alternating with blocks of geometric cross motives which can be hooked hit and miss.

#560A—Rose of Sharon 25″ x 36″ $3.00.
Same as #560.

#560B—Rose of Sharon 7′8″ x 10′5″ $35.00.
Same as #560.

#561—Celestial Wreath 37″ x 73″ $7.50.
Wreath of roses, black-eyed Susans, bluebells, lilies, tulips, marigolds. Spray of similar flowers at each end. Overlapping scrolls like cumulus clouds.

#562—Kingston 36″ x 56″ $5.25.
Center—two roses and cone flower. Poppies, morning-glories, coreopsis, bell flowers, and tulips. Simple curling scrolls terminating in three-leaf motives. Companion scroll to #552.

#563—Arum Lilies 30″ x 58″ $5.25.
Center—three roses, peony and buds, tulips, arum

lilies, crocus. Border of simple scrolls. Rose and buds in each corner, also at each end.

#564—Sumac Garlands 30" x 76" (30" x 6'4") $7.00.
Semi-conventional runner. Stylized four-petal flower motives, sprays of sumac leaves.

#565—Wild Ducks 26½" x 56" $5.25.
Pair of wild ducks on shore of pond under overhanging foliage. Corner scrolls. Copy of an old rug.

#566—Pilgrim 7'7½" x 9'7" (91½" x 115") $35.00.
Good dining-room pattern without center. An 18-inch outer border of large graceful flowing scrolls. Inner border of simpler scrolls and flower motives. Copy of an old rug.

#567—Old New England 7'8½" x 10'10" $37.50.
Center—mixed flowers enclosed in oval of simple scrolls. This in turn is surrounded by an oval of heavier scrolls with repeating flower motives. Clusters of mixed flowers fill corners. Entire rug surrounded by wide heavily veined scrolls.

#568—Plumes 9'3" x 10'4" Oval $45.00.
Small center of mixed flowers framed in an oval of plume leaves. Similar large plume leaves around outer edge. Diamond motives fill area between two ovals of plume leaves.

#569—Salem 45" x 83" $10.50.
Center—large flowers including salpiglosses, rudbeckia, trumpet flowers, petunias, roses, marigolds, tulips, Johnny-jump-ups. Knobby scrolls. Can be hooked oblong or oval.

#570—April 37" Round $4.00.
Two bunnies joyously smelling a tulip. Arched branches of bell flowers, and bluebirds form the setting. A child's rug.

#571—Bambi 37" Round $4.00.
A startled fawn in a clearing, surrounded by rhododendron leaves. A child's rug.

#572—Flip and Flop 37" Round $4.00.
Two cocker spaniels. A child's rug.

#573—Godey Spray 18" x 30" $2.00.
Two intertwining sprays of scroll leaves with clusters of berries between the scrolls. From an old Godey Book.

#574—Sunshine 18" x 30" $2.00.
One-way pattern without center. Poppies and cornflowers.

#575—Sweetbriar 18" x 30" $2.00.
A symmetrical garland spray of roses, poppies and star flowers.

#576—Romance 25½" x 37" $3.00.
Center—orange blossom, wild rose, single dahlia, tigridia, trumpet flowers, bitter-sweet, and bell flowers. Border of orange blossoms and leaves.

#577—Candlelight 24" x 37" $3.00.
Center—roses and buds, bell flowers, and five petal flowers. Small double-edge scroll gracefully interspersed with flowers. Leaves and five petal flowers in corners.

#578—Noel 24" x 37" $3.00.
Center—Christmas roses, crocuses, snowdrops. Unusual leaf border.

#579—Wedgwood Tile 26½" x 42½" $3.50.
Repeat pattern of 8-inch block motives of interlocking cross design. Plain 1¼-inch border.

#579A—Wedgwood Tile 34½" x 74½" $7.25.
Same as #579.

#579B—Wedgwood Tile 40" x 88" $10.50.
Same as #579, except that this size is printed without border.

#580—Tapestry Panel 14" x 30" or 36" $1.75.
Old English tapestry design of dahlias, tulips and bell flowers.

#581—Sun-Gay Footstool 22" x 22" $1.25.
Circle of flowers, 16 inches in diameter—lily, hibiscus and dahlia surrounded by calla-lily, pansy, morning-glory and tulip.

#582—Oyster-Bay Antique 37" x 63½" $6.50.
Two cornucopias spilling flowers and trailing ivy vines. Small central floral wreath. Copy of an old rug.

#583—Violets-Are-Blue Stool 17" x 23" $1.00.
Floral wreath 13" x 17" of roses and violets and buds.

#584—Joyous Stool 15" x 23" $1.00.
Single roses, buds and leaves. Framed with simple scroll.

#585—Oh! Susannah 27" x 38" $3.00.
Center—roses, morning-glories, and tulips. Simple leaf scroll.

#586—Early Spring 18" x 40" $2.00.
Single rose with leaves, trillium fern, dog-tooth violets, shooting stars, Dutchman's-breeches, and bleeding hearts. Fine trailing vine border. Design reverses.

#587—Century-Old Afghan 36" x 45½" Oval $4.50.
Center—three calla-lilies, two roses and buds, and morning-glories. Border—a wreath of the same flowers.

#588—Mosaic Sidewalk 19½" x 31½" $2.00.
A geometric design of one-inch blocks.

#589—Morning-Glory Stool 15" x 19½" $1.00.
Morning-glories, leaves and half-opened buds.

#590—Sudbury 30" x 48" $4.50.
Symmetrical center of roses. Border of stylized double-petaled flowers and four-leaf sprays. Cluster of leaves at each end. Copy of an old rug.

#591—Priscilla Alden 36" x 56" $5.25.
Center—one large rose with six large rose leaves, two rosebuds, and three simple five-petal flowers. Most unusual scroll with center vein and auxiliary veins running to scroll tips and terminating in tiny circles. Heavy scroll dominates small floral center. Copy of an old rug.

#592—Windswept 37" x 65" $6.50.
Center—four roses symmetrically grouped, rose leaves and buds, two five-petal flowers. C scrolls form a diamond and corners have three individual leaf sprays. Copy of an old rug.

#593—Gabriel 36" x 62" $6.25.
Center—four roses symmetrically grouped, rosebuds, and two five-petal flowers. Graceful scroll border. Copy of an old rug.

#594—Cameo 44" x 80" $10.00.
Center—large dahlia or daisy surrounded by roses, daisies and bell flowers. Unique border of leaf forms. Copy of an old rug.

#595—Peacock Feathers 30" x 45" $4.25.
Center—wreath of two roses and two zinnias. Scroll leaf border with "eyes" like peacock feathers. Good scroll for beginners. Copy of an old rug.

#596—Honesty 26" x 45" $4.25.
Symmetrical center of two four-petal flowers, tulip flowers and honesty. Heavy scroll border dominates small floral center. Copy of an old rug.

#597—Crested Wreath Antique 34" x 60" $5.75.
Double-edged branching leaf scrolls form an arch over

a bouquet of three roses, buds and leaves. One-way pattern. Copy of an old rug.

#598—Evangeline 36″ x 72″ $7.50.
Large scrolls almost entirely cover rug. Two long-stemmed roses and bud in each corner. Copy of an old rug.

#599—Sleepy Hollow Antique 37″ x 72″ $7.50.
Center—roses, lilies, and tulips. Compound leaf garlands form an oval around center motive. Corners—roses and buds. Copy of an old rug.

#600—Fleur-de-lis 45″ x 97½″ $14.50.
Center—roses, iris, lilies, narcissus, and four-o'clocks. Sprays of roses and four-o'clocks at both ends. Leafy ruffled scrolls with roses and four-o'clocks in corners.

#601—Periwinkle 46″ Round $6.25.
Assorted floral border 12 inches wide. Plain center.

#602—Clematis 37¾″ x 65″ Oval $6.50.
Center—different varieties of clematis. Feathery ruffled scrolls.

#603—Fuchsia 23¼″ x 37½″ $3.00.
Half round with word WELCOME. Ruffled petunias in corners, arching branches of fuchsias, buds and leaves.

#604—Interwoven Wreath 20″ x 34″ $2.75.
Extremely simple beginner's rug. Medallion center with two single roses and buds. Corners—three leaves and simple scrolls.

#605—Fall Foliage Stair Carpet 27″ wide $2.75 per yd.
Sumac leaves and fruit, oak leaves and acorns, maple leaves and winged fruit. Stocked in 2 yd. and 3 yd. lengths.

#606—Mr. & Mrs. Currier 24″ x 38″ $3.00.
Two figures in a horse-drawn sleigh. Also known as The Road Winter.

#607—Anemones 36½″ x 54½″ $5.00.
Center—anemones, calla-lilies, phlox, and bell flowers. Scalloped feathery scroll.

#608—Firefly 37″ Round $4.00.
Center—lily, rose, petunia, morning-glories, rose-haws, lily of the valley, honeysuckle, and phlox. Simple leaf scroll.

#609—Peg-o'-My-Heart 33″ x 60″ $6.00.
Center—single rose, lily and dahlia. Tulips and bell flowers. Heavy scroll similar to #596.

#610—Ariel 27″ x 42″ $3.75.
Center—bouquet of phlox, Johnny-jump-ups, lily of the valley, bell flowers, and rosebuds. Simple antler scroll. Good beginner's pattern.

#611—Peeking Pansies 37″ x 63″ $6.50.
Scrolls starting from center encompass the pattern. Pansies are tucked in corners and between scrolls.

#612—Beth's Bouquet 30″ x 51½″ $4.75.
Center—rose flanked by shamrocks and thistles. Unusual scroll arrangement.

#613—Pansies for Thought 27″ x 38″ $3.00.
Large pansies, buds, leaves and bowknots form border. Plain center.

#614—Elephant Ears 30″ x 50″ $4.75.
Center—montbretia, caladium leaves, zephyr lilies, summer hyacinths and morning-glories. Same flowers in border.

#615—Cat and Kittens 27″ x 54″ $5.00.
Cat with two kittens. Scroll corners. Old Frost pattern.

#616—Landscape Fruit & Flowers 36″ x 49½″ $5.50.
Vase of flowers on table containing fruits. Landscape background. Lattice with trumpet vine borders one side. *Currier & Ives* by Peters, color plate #39.

#617—Turanian 37″ x 76″ $8.00.
Persian design.

#618—Tea Rose 25″ x 30″ $2.75.
Single large hybrid tea rose, buds and leaves. Framed with simple band scroll.

#619—Pastel 36″ x 56″ $5.50.
Center—realistic spring flowers: lilies, tulips, and daffodils. Border of same flowers with the addition of iris and pussy willows.

#620—Dream Garden 45″ x 83″ Oval $11.00.
Elaborate floral rug. Center—poppies, petunias, phlox, morning-glories, frangipani, trumpet vine, anemones, nasturtiums, balloon flowers. Border—same flowers.

#621—Waltham Rose 29¾″ x 43″ $3.75.
Center—polyanthus roses and buds. Border is formed by simple bands interweaving sprays of single roses.

#622—Hallelujah 37″ x 54″ $5.50.
Flowing design of realistic roses, buds and leaves. Plain center.

#623—Kiss of the Sun. 24½″ x 42½″ $3.50.
Simple pattern. Morning-glory panel with narrow border of buds and leaves.

#624—Provincial 42″ x 94″ $11.50.
Block pattern of Pennsylvania Dutch and associated motives.

#625—Ruffles 36″ x 72″ $7.50.
An elaborate design. Center—peonies, parrot tulips, orchids, honeysuckle, Shirley poppies, ruffled petunias, and sweet peas. Feathery ruffled scrolls.

#626—Pungent Pine 25″ x 35″ $3.00.
Pine branches with cones.

#626A—Pungent Pine 35″ x 54″ $5.50.
Same as #626.

#626B—Pungent Pine 84″ x 84″ $23.00.
Same as #626.

#626C—Pungent Pine 72″ x 132″ $30.00.
Same as #626.

#626D—Pungent Pine 8′6″ x 11′ $46.00.
Same as #626.

#626E—Pungent Pine 25″ x 72″ $6.00.
Same as #626.

#627—Folk Art 36″ x 58″ $5.75.
Block pattern of Pennsylvania Dutch and associated motives.

#628—Iris 37″ x 54″ $5.50.
Flowing design of various types of iris, buds and leaves. Plain center. Companion to #622.

#629—Harmony 9′ x 12′ $50.00.
Heavily scrolled rug with pleasing mixed flower center. Outer scroll similar to scroll of #567.

#629A—Harmony 9′ x 15′ $62.50.
Same as #629.

#630—Duet 7′ x 9′ $30.00.
Small edition of Harmony—without the "heavy bass" outer scroll.

#631—Bridal Veil Falls 30″ x 47″ $4.75.
Currier & Ives—Yosemite. Illustrated in color in *Currier & Ives' America*, Crown Publishers, New York, 1952.

#632—Rose Trio Stool 27″ x 27″ Round or Square $2.00.
Center motive of three roses, buds, leaves—14½″ in diameter.

#633—Harebell Oval   26″ x 30″ $2.75.
Bell flowers gracefully turn around edge—flowers, buds and leaves in center. Good rug for thresholds.

#634—Litchfield Antique   20″ x 36½″ $2.75.
Very quaint old design with saw-tooth border and sprays of old-time flowers—mainly carnations.

#634A—Litchfield Antique   28″ x 40¾″ $3.75.
Same as #634.

#635—Rose of China   27″ x 59″ $5.25.
All-over pattern featuring camellias, buds and leaves on prominent boughs.

#636—Rose of China Stair Carpet   27″ wide $2.75 per yd.
Same design as above. This pattern may be cut at any point and be used as a runner. Stocked in 2 yd. and 3 yd. lengths.

#637—Fern Silhouette Stair Carpet   23½″ wide $2.75 per yd.
Fern's silhouette forms a background for spring flowers—dog-tooth violets, wild columbine, trillium and Dutchman's-breeches. Border of unfurling fern "fiddle heads." For narrower carpet border may be omitted. Stocked in 2 yd. and 3 yd. lengths.

#638—Fern Silhouette   23½″ x 48″ $4.00.
Same design as #637.

#639—Poppy Seed   27″ x 43″ $3.75.
Poppies, buds and leaves. Plain center.

#640—Poppy Square   52″ x 52″ $8.50.
Same design as #639.

#641—Chippendale Upholstery Seat   24″ x 22″ $1.50.
Design adapted from Chippendale tapestry seat. Scroll border—floral center.

#641A—Chippendale Upholstery Back   18″ x 24″ $1.00.
Same floral center as in seat—adaptable to many chair shapes and sizes.

#642—Butterfly Upholstery Seat   19″ x 17″ $1.00.
Spray of roses and buds with butterfly on branch.

#643—Dahlia Medallion   27″ x 37″ $3.00.
Simple scroll border. Flower center. Two single dahlias and two single chrysanthemums.

#644—Patricia   27″ x 37″ $3.00.
Ivy bordered rug. No center.

#645—Poppy Print   25″ x 30″ $2.75.
Companion to Tea Rose—poppies, buds and seed pods.

#646—Forest and Garden   31¼″ x 51½″ $4.75.
Oval. Roses grouped with pine and pine cones, no border.

#646A—Forest and Garden   36″ x 55½″ $5.50.
Same as #646 but oblong with border similar to Tea Rose.

#647—Rosebud Stool   18″ x 24″ $1.00.
A wreath of rosebuds.

#648—Mikado   25″ x 30″ $2.75.
Companion to Tea Rose—same frame border. Center —large chrysanthemum and leaves.

#649—Iceland Poppy   64″ x 78″ $18.00.
Same design as #640, longer and wider inner circle with conventionalized wheat motive—plain center.

#650—Star of the East   28½″ x 37″ $3.00.
Pictorial—three Wise Men on horseback following the Christmas Star.

#651—Abundance   54″ x 72″ $13.50.
Double border of mixed fruits. No center motive. Good dinette rug.

#652—Jewel Box   36½″ x 48½″ $5.00.
Wreath of mixed flowers framed by jewel-encrusted filagree—roses, tulips, daffodils, morning-glories, phlox, lilies, poppies, lilac, bluebells, carnations, apple blossoms, marigold, nicotiana, single dahlia.

#653—American Beauty   37″ x 73½″ $8.00.
Narrow interlocking scroll. Center—hybrid roses with fine sprays of forget-me-nots, bluebells, lily of the valley and lilac.

#654—Morning Dew   18″ x 30″ $2.00.
Spray of morning-glories with butterfly hovering over.

#655—June Morn   18″ x 30″ $2.00.
Center motive of mixed flowers, fuchsias, forget-me-nots, roses and rosebuds.

#656—Summertime   19″ x 30″ $2.00.
Half round, featuring poppies, wheat, bachelor-buttons, harebells, buttercups, daisies and clover.

#657—Lily Pool   36″ x 65″ $6.75.
Lacy scroll inspired by rhubarb leaf. Center—water lilies, buds, peonies and buds, carnations, bluebells, goldenrod.

#658—Corsage   36″ x 72″ $7.75.
Aubusson scroll in alternate corners, corsage of roses in opposite corners.

#659—Half Moon   36″ x 62″ $6.00.
Half-round rug with wide border motive of roses, buds, wild roses and forget-me-nots.

#660—Mandalay   35″ x 74″ $8.00.
Graceful hanging branches of wisteria and plum blossoms with birds.

#661—Mozart   13″ x 30″ $1.75.
Piano bench or fireside stool cover. Panel of various types of roses.

#662M—Temple Floor   24″ x 36″ $3.00.
Geometric, consisting of eight pointed stars with cross between. Adaptable to hit and miss.

#662A—Temple Floor   36″ x 72″ $7.50.
Same as #662M.

#663—Wildwood   68″ x 84″ $22.00.
A composition of wild forest motives—carpet of the forest having dried oak leaves, acorns, pine cones, ferns, mushrooms, jack-in-the-pulpits, dog-toothed violets, columbine, arbutus and lady-slippers.

#663A—Wildwood   84″ x 84″ $26.00.
Same as #663.

#663B—Wildwood   84″ x 108″ $30.00.
Same as #663.

#664—Swirl   60″ x 68″ $17.50.
Swirling, rampant scrolls with cat-o'-nine-tails, and jack-in-the-pulpits.

#665—Tea for Two   34″ x 68″ $7.00.
Large tea rose and bud, reversed and repeated at opposite end.

#666—Spring Serenade   45″ x 90″ $12.00.
Border of flamboyant tulips and iris.

#667—Peking   45″ x 72″   9.00.
Copy of a rare old Chinese rug.

#668—Thanksgiving   7′8″ x 10′ (92″ x 120″) $35.00.
Four corner horns of plenty spilling a graceful array of fruits and vegetables. Grape vine with grape clusters twining between horns of plenty.

#668A—Thanksgiving   9′ x 12′ $50.00.
Same as #668.

#668B—Thanksgiving   7′8″ x 8′7″ $30.00.
A dinette size of this handsome design.

HEIRLOOM RUG PATTERNS

#669—Tropical Lilies 27" x 37" $3.00.
Graceful narrow reedlike scrolls. Center—three tropical water lilies with buds and lily pads. Lily colors—blue, lavender-blue, amaranth pink, Egyptian white, rich apricot, coppery bronze.

#670—Flaming Oak 27" x 37" $3.00.
Graceful border of overlapping oak leaves and acorns, to be interpreted in either autumnal hues or summer greens. No center motive.

#671—Sunburst 27" x 37" $3.00.
Narrow, curling scrolls. Center—one large tea rose with buds and leaves.

#672—Four Dozen Roses 34" x 65" $6.75.
Each quarter consists of a spray of one dozen rosebuds.

#672A—Four Dozen Roses 45" x 72" $9.50.
Same as #672.

#673—Listen to the Mockingbird 45" x 88" $12.00.
Southern magnolia, buds and leaves with two mockingbirds on ends.

#674—Persian Stool 14" x 30" or 36" $2.00.
Oriental Pear or Mango motive.

#675—Mecca (Oriental) 54" x 89" $17.50.
Turkish Oriental design which fills the need for a rug larger than Frost's Oriental.

#676—Acanthus Border Oval 60" x 92" $20.00.
Wide graceful acanthus scroll. Floral center consisting of center roses, tulips, bluebells, lilies, marigolds, star flowers, morning-glories and pansies.

#677—Rose Upholstery Seat 22" x 24" $1.50.
Three large roses, bleeding hearts and lily of the valley with chippendale scroll.

#678—Browknot Upholstery Seat 22" x 24" $1.50.
Tulips, pansies and fuchsias tied with a bowknot.

#679—Joan of Arc 36½" x 64" $6.75.
Feathery scroll. Center motive—semi-double camellias with iris.

#680—Nature's Pets 30" x 51" $4.75.
Narrow flowing scroll. Floral center—dogwood and pussy willows.

#681—Kimberley 34" x 57½" $5.75.
All-over pattern of small diamonds with large center diamond framing three large tea roses, buds and leaves.

#681A—Kimberley 34" x 120" $13.00.
Same as #681. By cutting ends you can have a runner of any precise length.

#682—The Pup 24" x 36" $3.00.
Terrier pup with ball. Border—an intertwined leash with bells.

#683—Persian Palm Stair Carpet 27" wide $2.75 per yard.
Traditional Persian mango, river-loop, or pear motives cover field. Oriental motive in the border. Stocked in 2 yd. and 3 yd. lengths.

#683A—Persian Palm 36½" x 71" $8.00.
A scatter rug of same design as above.

#684—Chatterbox 37" Round $4.00.
Lovable gray squirrel on limb of oak tree with acorns and oak leaves, and vine of bittersweet berries.

#685—Leaf Upholstery Seat 24" x 22" $1.50.
Ornate wreath of leaves surrounding leafy branches.

#686—Colonial House 25½" x 41" $3.50.
Front view of colonial cottage with foundation planting of hollyhocks and shrubs.

#687—Leaflet 18½" x 31" $2.50.
Simple design of overlapping leaves. Good beginner's pattern.

#688—Freesia Border 37" x 66" $6.75.
Center—two lilies, two poppies, and mixed small flowers. Border—freesia flowers, buds and leaves interwoven with single roses.

#689—Broken Wreath 27" x 57" $5.25.
Center—open wreath of roses, cornflowers, and Canterbury bells—balanced at each end with similar treatment of the same flowers.

#690—Cathedral Windows 38" x 74" $7.50.
Versatile geometric, 12-inch motives.

#690A—Cathedral Windows 6'8" x 9'8" $30.00.
Same as #690.

#691—18th Century Mosaic Tile 38" x 74" $7.50.
Challenging geometric, 12-inch motives.

#692—Primroses 36" x 61" $5.75.
Center medallion of mixed flowers with primroses predominating. Ornate scroll.

#693—Hollyhock Welcome 25" x 41½" $3.00.
Half round. Quaint old design with lattice arched over three spires of hollyhocks.

#694—Flower Garden 39" x 56" $5.25.
Center—three roses accenting large medallion of mixed flowers. Unusual light scroll.

#695—Poppies 52" x 52" $8.50.
Center motive—eight sprays of poppies arranged in circular form. Light scroll encircles center. Can be hooked either square or round.

#696—Castles in Spain 48" x 72" $10.00.
Copy of handsome antique tapestry—bold treatment of an early American landscape and a medieval vision.

#697—U.S.A. Welcome 28" x 40" $3.50.
Half round. The great seal of the United States within a star border.

#698—Naval Welcome 25" x 39" $3.50.
Half round. Naval officer's insignia within a rope border.

#699—Johnny-Jump-Ups 27" x 38" $3.00.
Center—mixed small flowers including Johnny-jump-ups, roses, poppies, Canterbury bells, morning-glories, phlox. Simple scroll.

#700—Sweet Peas—28" x 37" $3.00.
Center—massed sweet peas. Border—graceful band of sweet-pea flowers, buds, and vines.

#701—Elephant 24" x 36" $3.00.
Chubby little nursery character—block border.

#702—Open Hearth 36" x 67" $6.75.
One-way hearth rug. Massed roses and buds, morning-glories, etc., framed in an arch of the same flowers.

#703—Chinese Dragons 36" x 42" $4.25.
Center—neutral Chinese motive. Corners—dragon motives.

#704—Chinese 34" x 60" $5.75.
Center similar to #703. Wide border, and inside corner motives.

#705—Dearborn Antique 36" x 54" $5.00.
Small center medallion of roses and mixed flowers. Heavy scroll inside banded border.

#706—Mardi Gras 30" x 52½" $4.75.
Semi-conventional. Geometric blocks frame woodcut flower and fleur-de-lis alternately.

#707—Daffodil Border 8'3" x 10'3" $40.00.
Center of mixed flowers in a field predominantly floral.

109

Outer border of light scrolls framing bouquets of daffodils and other flowers. This pattern is printed on three strips of 40-inch burlap for those who want to use a small frame.

#708—Moss Roses 45″ x 63″ $7.00.
Old-fashioned oval center of mixed flowers with four large roses and buds predominating. Graceful light scroll. Adaptation of an old rug. Kent II, plate 113, page 86.

#709—Painted Panel 36½″ x 96″ $11.50.
Rectangular panel of spring flowers framed in border of simple small scrolls.

#710—Rosette 28¾″ x 46½″ $4.00.
Banded medallion motives alternating with dainty rosettes.

#710A—Rosette 37¾″ x 64½″ $6.75.
Same as #710.

#711—Orchard Bough 20″ x 29″ $2.25.
Bough of apples and leaves.

#712—Small and Simple Series. Each 25″ x 34″ $3.00.
A group of small patterns the centers of which constitute only one species of flower or fruit—ideal for the beginner but tastefully qualified to satisfy the requirements of the advanced hooker. The same simple band scroll is used for all.

712A—Open Rose	712I—Fuchsia
712B—Talisman	712J—Clematis
712C—Cabbage Rose	712K—Daffodil
712D—Blueflag	712L—Poppy
712E—Pansy	712M—Pine
712F—Tulip	712N—Strawberry
712G—Morning-Glory	712O—Grape
712H—Lily & Viola	

#713—Oriental Runner 24½″ x 118″ $11.50.
13½-inch center panel of fine details. Triple border of graceful Oriental motives.

#714—Woven Ribbons 36″ x 69½″ $6.75.
Geometric—3-inch ribbons woven on the diagonal.

#714A—Woven Ribbons 23¼″ x 36″ $3.00.
Same as #714.

#715—Maple Leaf Diamond 40″ x 63″ $6.50.
Narrow diagonal bands form diamonds in each of which is dropped a large maple leaf.

#716—Heroic and Primitive Series
A group of early American designs with the same feeling of exaggerated simplicity that exists in contemporary design. Admirably suited for use with either colonial or modern furnishings.

#716A—Heroic Rose 40½″ x 74″ $8.00.
Two reversing sprays of very large roses, buds, and leaves. Wide frame border.

#716B—Canna Heroic 25″ x 55″ $5.00.
Graceful bold treatment of heroic flowers and buds. One-way rug.

#716C—Cornucopia Heroic 35″ x 70″ $7.00.
Sweeping treatment of heroic flowers, buds, and leaves giving cornucopia effect. Split-block border.

#716D—Marigold Heroic 28″ x 62½″ $6.00.
Well-balanced, rather full treatment of heroic flowers, buds, and leaves. Narrow plain border.

#716E—Acorn Heroic 36″ x 72½″ $7.00.
Large elliptical medallion of acorns and leaves.

#716F—Cabbage Rose Heroic 36″ x 68″ $6.50.
Center—very large exaggerated cabbage rose—flanked at each end of pattern with large crossed leaves. Triple-band border.

#716G—Crossed Rose Heroic 34½″ x 65½″ $6.50.
Crossed stems of large roses, buds, and leaves. Lamb's-tongue border.

#716H—Primitive Scenic Panel 25″ x 70″ $6.50.
A very simple center panel depicting an early American home and yard. Border of primitive flowers and leaves.

#716I—Primitive House 25″ x 46″ $4.25.
Center section of #716H

#716J—Indian Mosaic 32½″ x 45½″ $4.25.
Block pattern—blocks containing primitive flowers, berries, or leaves.

#716K—Mountaineer's Cabin 37″ x 45″ $4.25.
Primitive scene of cabin and door yard nestled on the mountainside.

#716L—Sailcloth Primitive 29″ x 68½″ $6.50.
Graceful treatment of primitive flowers and leaves. Copy of a very old rug—hooked by a sailor on sailcloth.

#716M—Indian Chief Panels 37″ x 75″ $7.50.
Primitive geometric of five panels. The outer panels are shells or lamb's-tongues, the adjacent panels imply channels of rippling water and eddies, and the center panel consists of straight-line stepped mountains.

#716N—Indian Squaw Panels 34″ x 63″ $6.00.
Primitive geometric of five panels. The two outside panels and the center panel consist of straight-line peaks, and the adjacent panels imply the curving course of water lapping a ragged shore.

#716O—Horn of Plenty Heroic 33″ x 64″ $5.75.
Swirling cornucopias spilling flowers and leaves.

#717—Sylvan Fretwork 36½″ x 73″ $7.50.
Oval. Interlacing oak leaf and acorn tracery design. Similar to center of #516—White Oak.

#718—Of Thee I Sing 45″ x 69″ $10.00.
A pictorial map of the U.S.A., generously illustrating points of national interest and products or historical progress typical of the individual states.

#719—Plume Leaf 27″ x 54″ $5.00.
Plain center framed by handsome leaf border.

#719A—Plume Leaf 27″ x 90″ $8.00.
#719B—Plume Leaf 27″ x 126″ $11.00.
#719C—Plume Leaf Stair Carpet 27″ $2.75 per yd.
Stocked in 2 yd. and 3 yd. lengths.

#720—Old Covered Bridge 27½″ x 38″ $3.75.
A peaceful rural scene of rare design. A colored print is supplied with each pattern.

#721—Old Grist Mill 29½″ x 38″ $3.75.
The original Millbourne Mill of Cobb's Creek, Philadelphia. A colored print is supplied with each pattern.

#722—Yorktown 45½″ x 75½″ $9.50.
Copy of an old Aubusson carpet in the Moore Farmhouse at Yorktown. It was in this historic house that terms of surrender offered by General Cornwallis were accepted by the officers of General Washington. Alternate 15-inch floral and geometric motives form an all-over pattern of great dignity and appeal.

#723—Harvest Moon 42″ x 72″ $9.00.
Two reversed cornucopias spilling a graceful array of harvest fruits and vegetables.

#724—Plenty 36″ x 56″ $5.50.
A handsome center medallion of various fruits framed in a graceful border of grapevines and grapes.